CRIME AND TECHNOLOGY
New Frontiers for Regulation, Law Enforcement and Research

CRIME AND TECHNOLOGY

NEW FRONTIERS FOR REGULATION, LAW ENFORCEMENT AND RESEARCH

EDITED BY

ERNESTO U. SAVONA

Professor of Criminology, Università Cattolica del Sacro Cuore, Milan, Italy
Director of Transcrime, Joint Research Centre on Transnational Crime,
Università degli Studi di Trento - Università Cattolica del Sacro Cuore, Italy

 Springer

Library of Congress Cataloging-in-Publication Data is available.

ISBN 978-90-481-6746-3 (PB)
ISBN 978-1-4020-2924-0 (e-book)   ISBN 1-4020-2924-1 (e-book)

Published by Springer,
P.O. Box 17, 3300 AA Dordrecht, The Netherlands

Sold and distributed in North, Central and South America
by Springer,
101 Philip Drive, Norwell, MA 02061, U.S.A.

In all other countries, sold and distributed
by Springer,
P.O. Box 322, 3300 AH Dordrecht, The Netherlands

Printed on acid-free paper

Printed in the Netherlands.

TABLE OF CONTENTS

FOREWORD

Guido Rossi

As Chairman of ISPAC, I want to thank all the contributors to this book that originates from the International Conference on Crime and Technology. This could be the end of my presentation if I did not feel uneasy not considering one of the problems I believe to be pivotal in the relationship between crime and technology. I shall also consider that the same relationship exists between terror and globalization, while globalization is stemming from technology and terror from crime. Transnational terrorism is today made possible by the vast array of communication tools. But the paradox is that if globalization facilitates terrorist violence, the fight against this war without borders is potentially disastrous for both economic development and globalization. Antiterrorist measures restrict mobility and financial flows, while new terrorist attacks could lead the way for an antiglobalist reaction.

But the global society has yet to agree on a common definition of terrorism or on a common policy against it.The ordinary traditional criminal law is still depending on the sovereignty of national states, while international criminal justice is only a spotty and contested last resort. The fragmented and weak international institutions and underdeveloped civil societies have no power to enforce criminal justice against terrorism. At the same time, the states that are its targets have no interest in applying the laws of war (the Geneva Conventions) to their fight against terrorists. Wars are supposed to begin and to end and to be declared and fought against a state. But terrorism had no precise beginning and nobody knows when the bitter end will occur. Furthermore there is no such state called Terror where terrorists abide, while Al-Qaeda is almost a nation. The states have every interest in treating terrorist as outlaws and pariahs, and when prisoners they are described, in the voice for example of the U.S. President, as killers. The prisoners at Guantanamo Bay are beyond the rule of law and in the words of Lord Johan Steyn, in a very important article, the whole situation constitutes "A Monstrous Failure of Justice" (*International Herald Tribune*, November 27, 2003). The problem of the Guantanamo Bay jurisdiction is now standing for judgment before the Supreme Court of the U.S.

We can analyze the present, but we cannot predict the future.

The present is that not having the possibility to enforce against terrorism either the internal criminal laws of the states, with all their procedural guarantees for a fair trial, or the international conventions on war, the terrorists in prison are deprived of their human rights.

The future is the challenge to find a new legal order to fight terrorism. We have to discuss and try to find the way out, asking politicians, civil society, historians, philosophers, sociologists, lawyers, scientists, and academic organizations to look for general accepted rules of human morality, whose principles cannot be subject to any trade-off, not even to fight terrorism. Those principles shall be the basis for new international Conventions to be submitted to the United Nations.

This is the challenge of the agenda of ISPAC for the near future. This challenge is a dilemma facing democracies, and to conclude I want to quote Aharon Barak, President of the Supreme Court of Israel (mentioned also in Lord Johan Steyn's article). In a case in which the Court held that violent interrogation of a suspected terrorist is not lawful even if doing so may save human life by preventing impending terrorist acts, he said: "Sometimes, a democracy must fight with one hand tied behind its back. Nonetheless, it has the upper hand. Preserving the rule of law and recognition of individual liberties constitute an important component of its understanding of security. At the end of the day, they strengthen its spirit and strength and allow it to overcome its difficulties" (*Case No. 5100/94, Public Committee Against Torture v. State of Israel*, July 15, 1999 [Available on the Israeli Supreme Court Internet Site]).

INTRODUCTION

Ernesto U. Savona

The chapters collected in this book are revised versions of the papers presented at the ISPAC international Conference on Crime and Technology held in Courmayeur on November 2003. Some of them have been selected and published in the *European Journal on Crime and Criminal Policy* of Kluwer. This book is a partial spin-off of the Journal. It aims to develop a better knowledge of the impact of technology on crime, either looking at how criminals change their *modus operandi*, or how legislation, law enforcement and research could help in developing better laws, qualified investigations, and more applied research.

It is well known from daily experience that criminals, either individually or in organised criminal groups, exploit technologies (with particular preference for ICT) in order to maximise opportunities and minimise the so-called "law enforcement risk", i.e. the risk of being detected, prosecuted, convicted, punished, and of having the proceeds of their crimes confiscated. The consequences of the exploitation of technology for criminal purposes can be summarized as follows:

- producing new opportunities for crime,
- facilitating/changing techniques and *modi operandi* for committing crimes,
- creating new crimes.

Conversely, it is likely that new technologies will have an increasing role in the fight against crime in the next years. Such role could be split in two main typologies of actions, categorised as follows:

- providing law enforcement agencies and criminal justice systems with new means to identify and prosecute criminals;
- developing technologies that help both citizens and businesses to reduce crime opportunities.

This situation raises issues which have to be addressed from different perspectives:

- Law enforcement agencies are changing their investigative techniques and their *modi operandi*. The use of CCTV, biometrics, and new forensic techniques, including the development and use of DNA databases, are only some examples of

technologies used in the fight against crime. Forensic science and technology will both be of special relevance in the development of law enforcement activities.
- National Governments and international institutions are asked to adapt their legal instruments to this new situation. Cybercrime conventions and laws are already in their agenda. In these regulations the traditional divisions between criminal and civil laws are blurred. Jurisdictional and procedural problems also arise when investigations of computer-related crimes (CRCs) are to be undertaken. Moreover, complex privacy issues are central to the debate about the trade off existing between security, justice and civil rights protection.
- New subjects are also entering the area of crime prevention and crime control. For example, the private sector is directly involved: not only does it produce technology but it is also the beneficiary when technologies are used in order to prevent crime and reduce the victimization rate. Academics themselves may share their expertise and the results of their research activities with policy makers, practitioners, professionals and law enforcement officials in order to develop the most effective and efficient solutions for combating and reducing crime.

All these issues need to be analyzed in order to gain knowledge of the phenomena and to approach the development of new frontiers of law, regulation and enforcement. These aims can be reached through the explication of specific tasks against high-tech crime and its implications, taking a critical look at existing legal frameworks at both the national and international levels and identifying gaps, issues and means to meet the challenge posed by a rapidly evolving situation. These could be summarized as follows:

1. developing new legal instruments against high-tech crime at both the national and international level;
2. improving law enforcement knowledge and expertise on both crime trends and the use of new instruments to reduce high-tech crime;
3. promoting and organizing training activities for prosecutors and judges in order to improve their knowledge of high-tech crimes and all the related legal issues;
4. improving co-operation and reinforcing partnerships against crime in order to enhance the sharing of information and knowledge;
5. developing research focusing on all the components of high-tech crime;
6. designing new curricula for professionals and university students introducing them to the civil and criminal legal implications of high-tech crime.

The chapters of the book follow these problems. Starting from some key questions that crime and technology poses at international level, the book proceeds by introducing the topic and outlining what is changing in committing crime and in combating it through IC technologies. Three steps are considered: legislation, law enforcement and research.

For the first, the analysis follows the lines of the international instruments available today, outlining how crucial it is to develop adequate national legislations for better and more effective international co-operation. For law enforcement, different aspects are considered: from the challenges law enforcement agencies meet today in developing their investigative techniques to the problems of collecting electronic evidence and the issue of compatibility between security needs and privacy rights.

Research is the third step considered by the book. Criminology has some difficulties in interpreting changes in crime and developing adequate responses. Rotating around the criminal justice systems, traditional criminology runs the risk of becoming mute in front of those crimes, such as cyber-crimes or cyber-related crimes, almost not reported. Criminal sanctions and prisons cannot be the instruments for fighting cyber-crime and criminals. Either as a new criminology, which takes care of reducing opportunities for crime, or as a recently named "crime science", researchers are today challenging the capability of science in producing analyses and solutions for reducing crime. This should be considered with attention by policy makers and law enforcement agencies.

The message the book sends to the international community is to develop close partnerships among different components of society for paying cumulative attention to the relationships between crime and technology. Making possible distortions of technology for criminal purposes could be controlled and reduced, to the advantage of a common welfare whose technology is an important component.

CHAPTER 1

EMERGING CHALLENGES

Antonio M. Costa

INTRODUCTION

The issue of technology and its misuse by criminals increasingly runs like a golden thread through all discussions of the new security threats that face the contemporary world.

What is perhaps so remarkable, and a critical element in why it is so difficult to understand the implications of these trends, is the speed at which these developments have occurred. The World Summit on the Information Society held in Geneva was confronted with a range of critical issues in this regard, including the thorny question of the governance of the internet itself.

In the space of only about ten years significant advances in the field of technology have transformed global information flows and the way in which business is conducted.

To take just one indicator: the growth of the internet – a key symbol of globalisation and the domain for the spread of information and the conducting of legitimate business transactions, but equally, providing significant new opportunities for cybercrimes such as fraud, the spread of pornographic material, the misuse of personal data and sabotage.

In 1991 there were only a handful of internet hosts or websites, but by the beginning of 2003, there were reported to be a minimum of 180 million. That is a truly phenomenal level of growth. What is perhaps more startling is that over half of that growth has taken place over the last three years with an estimated 100 million hosts being added in that short period.[1]

The benefits that such advances bring are significant – both for legitimate business activity, but also for those who engage in unlawful acts.

While terrorist organizations may still use bombs and bullets to kill and intimidate in order to promote their cause, technology has greatly facilitated these activities. Instructions for making explosive devices can be downloaded from the internet, and communication between secret cells takes place through the use of encrypted e-mails. Traffickers now not only transport tangible goods such as drugs or weapons, again using advances in technology to facilitate their underground trade, but they also traffic in 'intangible commodities' – such as child pornography – that can be shifted at the touch of a button.

---

1 Data collected by the Internet Systems Consortium, see <www.isc.org>.

Ernesto U. Savona (ed.), Crime and Technology: New Frontiers for Regulations, Law Enforcement and Research, 1–6.
© 2004 *Springer. Printed in The Netherlands.*

THE SCOPE OF THE CHALLENGE

As we try to anticipate the effects of technology's accelerated expansion, there are two important dimensions to consider.

Firstly, the use of technology has broadened from wealthy and sophisticated users to the wider population. There can be few businesses, organizations and households in the developed world which do not have access to the internet and do not use it for the conduct of their activities.

Secondly, even in the developing world the benefits brought by technological advances are not insignificant. Perhaps the best example of this is that in many poor and even war-torn states, where official systems of governance have all but collapsed, the mobile phone and e-mail are ubiquitous symbols of technological penetration.

This dual shift of the use of technology – both downwards and outwards – provides a critical space for the development of criminal opportunities that national frontiers can do little to contain. Take just one example that many of us have experienced – proposals for advanced fee fraud or '419 scams', the speciality of West African criminal groups, which generally involve the request for an upfront payment on the promise of a greater financial reward that never, of course, materializes. Originally such letters were faxed to a few hundred possible victims; now the internet has been used as a resource to identify likely targets, with electronic mail providing an ability to make contact with thousands of possible victims simultaneously.

There can be little doubt too that the spread of electronic banking and the rapid growth of the internet have resulted in new opportunities for economic and financial crimes. The global interdependence of the international financial system also accentuates the knock-on effects of unlawful activity. In prominent cases of substantial fraud in the banking system in the last decade, for example, such as that of BCCI, the implications were truly global, involving investors across the world and damaging the banking systems of a number of developing countries.

In a number of cases advances in technology have brought burgeoning new criminal industries.

Fraud using credit or debit cards is now acknowledged to be a serious international problem, generating higher levels of illicit profits than the counterfeiting of currency. While the growing use of plastic cards during the late 1970s and early 1980s saw various attempts at their fraudulent use, by the late 1990s this has become a truly globalised business with sophisticated organised crime groups making use of advanced counterfeiting technologies.

The anti-fraud manager of a major credit card company recently reported that it is now common – and making use of technologies that can often be purchased off the shelf – for data from genuine credit cards to be compromised in one country in the morning, counterfeit cards produced using the stolen data in the afternoon in a second country, then purchases made that evening in a third country. These countries may not even be on the same continent. In 2000 global losses for fraud committed using plastic cards was estimated to be in excess of US$ 2 billion (Vanhinsbergh, 2001).

Quite apart from the opportunities that technology provides for crimes aimed at profit, our reliance (you may perhaps even say over-reliance) on technology brings with it significant new dangers. Bluntly put, our dependence on technology means that it causes much greater harm when it fails or comes under threat.

Technology then may itself be the subject of attack for purposes of ideology or profit.

The reliance of the global financial system on high-tech communications systems makes it vulnerable to attack by those who may wish to disrupt it. And, because globalisation places such a high premium on the provision of information, this process too is subject to the age-old crime of extortion.

The last two months have seen a wave of cyber attacks on online web retailers, internet payment systems and online gambling sites. Payments from the companies involved were then extorted under the threat that the attacks would resume.

Law enforcement officials suggest that these attacks are not the work of mischievous hackers but of sophisticated criminal operations, which were traced back to Eastern Europe.

TOWARDS A GLOBAL RESPONSE

The impact of technology on crime crosses borders, and while we often debate the issue as one which impacts only upon the developed world, there are critical implications for developing countries.

If law enforcement agencies in the developed world struggle to retain skills and keep up with new technologies, how can similar agencies in countries in transition and in the developing world hope to compete?

This question becomes all the more urgent when it is taken into account that in many high-technology crimes the physical presence of the offender is not a defining factor. Crimes can therefore be committed from jurisdictions that have the weakest legal framework and law enforcement infrastructure to counter them. This highlights the degree to which there is a global community of interests in ensuring effective law enforcement capacity in the developing world, combined with effective systems for states to exchange information and intelligence and provide mutual legal assistance.

The United Nations has a key role to play in this regard. The UN Convention against Transnational Organized Crime, which entered into force in September of this year, provides a global response to the problems of criminal organizations and provides mechanisms for more effective cross-border cooperation. Nevertheless, this Convention only covers high-technology crimes perpetrated by organized criminal groups. Indeed, it has already been suggested that a specific international instrument to deal with the issue of high-tech criminality is now a prerequisite for building an effective global response.

Advances in technology in themselves provide critical mechanisms to facilitate greater global cooperation. It seems likely that over time law enforcement agencies from all parts of the globe will be in much greater electronic communication with each other. They will be able to access sophisticated global databases and track criminals more effectively across borders. The foundations for such a system are already in place through INTERPOL.

As always, however, it must be emphasised that any database or communication technology is only as good as the number of countries that would participate in such a system, as well as the quality of the information that is provided. Technology can enhance the work of law enforcement but cannot completely substitute for traditional policing or intelligence gathering methods.

TECHNOLOGIES FOR COMBATING CRIME:TRADE-OFFS AND CHALLENGES

Such wider access to information, the ease with which it can be collected, and its exchange among multiple agencies across the globe raise significant issues in respect of human rights. The threat of terrorism and the global reach of organized crime places renewed pressures on governments to ensure the safety of their citizens, and new demands by law enforcement and security personnel for more intrusive means to collect information to achieve this. The balance between the rights of states to access information, and the rights of citizens to their privacy, is surely one of the most important debates of the global information society.

This debate between privacy and accessibility to information demonstrates only too clearly that while technology brings many opportunities it also carries with it great challenges. For the most part, I suspect these are seldom different for law enforcement agencies than they are for any other business or government institution.

Key questions that managers have to ask themselves are, in the context of limited resources, which technologies are the most appropriate for their organization – the answers to this may not always be as obvious as they seem. A recent review of the technological requirements of local police departments in the United States based on a survey sent to many agencies came to a surprising conclusion: The technologies that police managers emphasised that needed upgrading were not necessarily the fancy law enforcement gadgets that the general public would have considered to be on the list, but rather better systems for administration and accounting (Schwabe et al., 2001).

Introducing technology into any workplace also requires a series of trade offs. Because of the labour intensity of most policing activities, technology acquisition almost always has to compete with a number of other priorities, from placing more patrol officers on the street to improving levels of service. And, because of the variety of ways in which law enforcement agencies can allocate their funds, it is trade offs amongst different technologies themselves that are likely to be important.

Rapid advances in technology pose an additional and important challenge – while providing technologies to a police agency today may introduce immediate benefits, the return of the investment will gradually decrease as the systems become obsolete, and are overtaken by other newer technologies. It is possible that other programmes, whose returns increase with time rather than decrease, might be better policy targets. Here the importance of training, an issue that must receive some attention. Correctly conducted, training has the possibility to improve not only how officials use current technologies, but also building capacity in order to improve their use of the technologies of the future, and, at the same time, building a better understanding of the implications of technology use on human rights.

None of the challenges or trade offs I have spoken of should be interpreted as a belief that technology is not bringing a revolution to law enforcement. If we are realistic, however, that revolution brings with it a series of questions about the most adequate application of technology, not only to enhance ordinary policing, but also more specialized law enforcement interventions. As I believe many authors will indicate, the use of DNA technology, advances in forensic science and improved capacities for intelligence collection will mean that police agencies, particularly in highly specialized fields, will continue to undergo rapid advances.

In the context of this debate it must be highlighted too that technology can play a critical role not only in improving the prospects for effective law enforcement, but also for improving the transparency and accountability of agencies responsible for bringing justice. More sophisticated information systems also mean that the monitoring of police performance is enhanced. These factors have resulted in greater scrutiny of the police, more public awareness about both their successes and failures, and greater pressures than ever on police managers to orientate their agencies towards more clearly stated goals and objectives.

Greater access to information in the longer term will also by implication improve the transparency of governments, a key prerequisite for fighting corruption.

CONCLUSIONS

The role of the United Nations is to provide assistance to developing countries and countries in transition. We need to continue to study the lessons learnt in the field of technological interventions to combat crime, enriching the input and advice we provide in the field of law enforcement and crime prevention.

There can be little doubt that advances in technology have both brought new opportunities for the conducting of criminal activity as well as new opportunities and challenges for law enforcement. It is perhaps not yet possible to fully understand the implications of these developments – hence the importance of maintaining a healthy debate that brings together not only government officials, but members of the scientific and academic communities as well as representatives of civil society, debating not only the specific details of the technologies themselves, but their broader implications for our communities.

REFERENCES

Schwabe, W., L.M. Davis, and B.A. Jackson, *Challenges and Choices for Crime-fighting Technology: Federal Support of State and Local Law Enforcement.* Santa Monica, California: The Rand Corporation, 2001.

Vanhinsbergh, S., Fraude aux cartes de paiement: l'évolution des pratiques. *Revue Internationale de Police Criminelle*, 491, pp.18–23, 2001.

CHAPTER 2

THE FOX AND THE HUNTERS: HOW IC TECHNOLOGIES CHANGE THE CRIME RACE*

Ernesto U. Savona and Mara Mignone

INTRODUCTION

What is the role and the impact of technologies on crime? Criminals use them for maximizing their opportunities and minimizing the risk of being detected and caught. The Police do exactly the reverse, using technologies for detecting crime and criminals and arresting them. The range of relationships between technologies and crime is wide. This paper focuses on a relatively narrow path: Information and Communication Technologies (ICT) related crime, looking at how criminals and law enforcement agencies use ICT.

Specifically, the paper aims at developing two aspects: an analysis of how new technologies are reshaping criminal typologies, dynamics and trends; and an analysis of the most important challenges that legislation, law enforcement and science have to face in order to prevent and combat ICT-related crime. In fact, evidence shows that there is an urgent need to improve knowledge about the phenomena, and develop new paradigms and theories together with best practices.

Each section opens with a specific question and develops by trying to find a suitable answer. We start by trying to analyse what impact new technologies have on society and crime. The paper continues by examining how criminal patterns are changing (*How do ICTs facilitate the commission of new and traditional crimes?*) and who these criminals are (*Are criminals really going cyber?*). It ends by focusing on the other side, on how crime is prevented and combated (*How are technologies reshaping the approach and the fight against crime at legal, law enforcement and scientific levels?*).

This chapter was previously published in *European Journal on Criminal Policy and Research* **10**: 3–26, 2004.
* This article is the result of the combined efforts of the two authors. Mara Mignone drafted the first version, which was then revised and finalised by Ernesto U. Savona.

Ernesto U. Savona (ed.), Crime and Technology: New Frontiers for Regulations, Law Enforcement and Research, 7–28.
© 2004 *Springer. Printed in The Netherlands.*

THE IMPACT OF NEW TECHNOLOGIES ON SOCIETY AND CRIME

What is the Impact of New Technologies on Both
Society and Crime?

The increasing attention (the word is used in the absence of reliable statistics) being paid to ICT-related crimes shows their exploitation for the commission of harmful and unlawful activities. While the internet and other information technologies are generating countless benefits for society, they also provide new opportunities for criminal behaviour.

The presence of ICT in modern societies is pervasive, which makes crime, especially ICT-related crime, a *'constituent aspect of the wider political, social and economic restructuring currently affecting countries worldwide'* (Thomas and Loader 2000). This is what is causing modern societies to become risk societies (Beck 1999).

Societies rely on technologies to organise and administer themselves, offer services to citizens, educate and communicate.[1] Economic globalisation is enhanced by new technologies, which provide opportunities in international markets. Multinational enterprises, and also small and medium companies, are carrying out their businesses more easily, without spatial barriers. Technologies allow them to invest in new activities or enter new markets and free them to invent new ways of presenting themselves and offering their services/goods. A boundless, unlimited flow of information, together with the possibility to establish international networks, facilitates the reduction of economic costs, and direct and indirect risks.

This is no different from what ICT allows criminals to do. They use new technologies to communicate, to organise themselves better, to widen the spectrum of their businesses, to update their *modus operandi* and techniques, and to avoid law enforcement risk.

Rational theories on crime (Becker 1974; Cornish and Clarke 1986) would explain this attitude towards new technologies as just a problem of maximizing benefits while reducing costs. It could be defined as a matter of *opportunities*. In fact, it is well known that criminals, either as individuals or organised, are able to reorganise and adapt to changes in the local and global environment. In recent years, for example, there has been a tendency for criminals to enter new markets and develop new, less risky activities (Adamoli et al. 1998). Technological developments in telecommunications, the networking of financial and banking systems, the increasing use of computers in the business sector, the globalisation of markets and, conversely, the lack of efficient and ready countermeasures on the part of law and law enforcement, are all factors that have increased opportunities and reduced risks for criminals.

Moreover, there is nothing very new or surprising in the adoption of new technologies by criminals. Earlier technological developments also brought about dramatic improvements for society, but also created new opportunities for misconduct.

---

1   Almost everything, from health-care services, transport, air traffic control, banking, telecommunications and the military rely on networked computers.

There are cases of criminals using portable radios to intercept police transmissions, or mobile phones (when they were still a rarity) to avoid the risk of being intercepted while communicating. However, as will be explained, the situation is a little different (and more serious) with the internet and ICTs.

To summarize, the scenario outlined above demonstrates that the impact of ICTs has produced relevant changes to crime and consequently to the law enforcement for detecting it. It is like a fox hunting where the fox (criminals) are frequently better-off than hunters (law enforcement).

A sort of wish list could help to explain why a criminal should use ICTs for his/her purposes (Brill 1999):

1. *ICTs clear each spatial hurdle and permit a global reach*. This means that criminals can get to their victims or conclude their affairs remotely. A good example is *cyberstalking*. This is analogous to traditional forms of stalking, as the result is to place another person in fear for his/her safety (Ogilvie 2000). However, with the advent of new technologies, traditional forms of stalking have been enriched with new variations, due to new mediums such as e-mail and the internet. In fact, the stalker can use chat-rooms, forums or personal web pages to find a victim and to collect information about him/her. Repeated, unwanted contacts with the victim can be established by sending e-mails, or even malicious code. Direct contacts are also possible *via* chat-rooms attended by the victim, whose channel can also be flooded by the stalker in order to inhibit conversation with other people. The end result may be a concrete violation of a victim's privacy or even personal assault, and the use of the victim's identity to commit fraud or other illegal behaviour. Another example could be *cyberlaundering*. New technologies, and especially the internet, are the technical framework that facilitates global money laundering, because they can be used for different purposes. First, to obtain false identity documents and passports, or obtain a new, valid identity, by means of all the numerous services offered over the Net. As regards the stages of the money laundering process, the opportunities for the criminals are manifold. For example, during the placement phase, 'virtual' accounts can be set up online in off-shore banks using only a photograph or fake documents. During the layering phase, dirty money can be withdrawn or transferred digitally from one account to another, from bank to bank, or invested in virtual casinos or other online activities. Exploiting the multi-jurisdictional nature of the internet, and the diversity of rules, criminals can also create businesses and front companies – i.e. all with their headquarters in off-shore countries – that could be used during the integration phase. In this way, they will give money the appearance of legitimate winnings or earnings. In this case, the interdependence between the virtual environment and reality is evident.

2. *ICTs are globally available*. Potentially, the internet can be accessed from anywhere, at any time. Worldwide statistics on Internet Domains (host numbers[2]) and

---

2   http://www.isc.org/ds/WWW-200207/index.html.

internet usage percentages show that they are both on the increase.[3] The internet is absent only in a small part of the globe. It is true that a large part of the world still has minimal (if any) access to communication networks. This is not the case with criminals, however. They can also use the different typologies of connections (dial-up, satellite phone, etc.) depending on the requirements of the criminal scheme.

3. *ICTs are generally speedy.* Technological solutions allow people, and also criminals, to have fast, permanent connections, which guarantee the continuous availability of the internet in particular.

4. *ICTs basically guarantee anonymity.* This could become a false myth if not explained properly. From a technological standpoint, with the exclusion of those cases where criminals are really highly skilled, each activity carried out using technology can be back-tracked.[4] In fact, forensic procedures allow almost all the operations carried out on a computer system/network to be uncovered. Among others, the problems are the concrete possibility of investigating all cases – which are mostly transnational – and to be able to associate a physical, personal identity to the computer used in the criminal scam. Moreover, the point is that the internet is intrinsically transnational. There are no clear rules and no country owns or controls it. Thus, anonymity may be both technical and legal.

5. *ICTs can be very secure.* In fact, the use of encryption, namely steganography and cryptography, protect the kinds of communications criminals need to send and any kind of document they want to 'hide' Software and tools are freely available over the internet, together with the instructions on how to use them.

6. *ICTs are characterized by multimedia capability.* They allow the use of different sources of information (hardware and software): texts, images, sounds, videos, recorded voice and real-time voice are only some examples. Digitalization has really opened the way to the communication revolution, and to abuse revolution too. This is the case with *intellectual property rights infringements,* and in partic- ular with on-line music piracy (Malagò and Mignone 2000). It is also the case with *on-line paedophilia* and *pedo-pornography* (Akdeniz 2001).

7. *ICTs are prevalently inexpensive.* In respect to other communication systems (i.e. phone and mobile phone), the cost of using the internet is very low.

8. *ICTs are easy to use.* They are based on a user-friendly, intuitive approach, so there is no need for special training.

9. *ICTs are still underregulated.* As will be explained in the second part of this con- tribution, the legal rules existing for ICT-related crime are still too fragmentary and embryonic (RAND Europe 2003). They are essentially incapable of preventing and repressing this type of crime.

---

3   http://www.gandalf.it/data/data1.htm.
4   This is the case of the Italian Operation Rootkit, led by the Financial Police. In August 2002, after a year of investigation, 14 Italian hackers – primarily information security professionals – were arrested and charged with hacking into the networks of NASA, the US Army, the US Navy and various universities around the world (Forte 2003).

10. *ICTs are difficult for law enforcement authorities to investigate*. This issue will also be addressed specifically in the second part of this contribution. Here, it is important to highlight that law enforcement is confronted by a really serious challenge, as ICT-related crimes are on the increase.

This is the scenario representing the impact of new technologies on crime. The following section enters into detail and explains why the ICT revolution can be defined as a veritable 'Pandora's box' of criminal offences and challenges.

ICT-RELATED CRIME: THE EXPLOITATION OF NEW TECHNOLOGIES FOR CRIMINAL PURPOSES

How Do ICTs Facilitate the Commission of
New and Traditional Crimes?

How technologies are exploited for criminal purposes and the role they play in facilitating crime can be schematized as follows (TRANSCRIME, 2002a: 25):

1. New technologies may be the *subject* of a crime.

    This happens when they form the environment in which the crime is planned and committed. The internet is a suitable environment where a crime can be designed, because it is a valuable source of information. Information is the essence of the internet itself, which can be defined as an enormous database embracing almost all fields of knowledge. Information is free, updated and is also easily attainable by those persons who are not very accustomed to PCs. This means that amongst all the things covered by the Net, there are also, for example, instructions on how to write malicious code, how to hack an information system or bypass the security solutions, which protect CDs or satellite transmissions. Instructions on how to prepare a nuclear bomb are also available. Internet is also the environment where toolkits to attack computer systems and data are normally uploaded and made accessible.

2. New technologies may be the object of a crime.

    This happens when the criminal act has an effect on technologies, so that they are the object (or target) of crime. Technically, these behaviours are called *computer crimes*,[5] or also CIA offences, which are all the offences against the confidentiality, integrity and availability of computer data and systems.[6] These are new,

---

5   It is worth underlining that there is still no agreement about the terms and the definitions used to classify computer crime. Very often, different terms and expressions are used as synonyms of computer crime. For example, computer crimes are also called cybercrimes or technocrimes.

6   Information security is particularly concerned with preserving the confidentiality, integrity and availability of an organisation's information. It can be defined as follows (definitions are taken from the Information Security Glossary, which can be retrieved at the following URL: http://www.yourwindow.to/ information-security/gl_confidentiality-integrityandavailabili.htm): Confidentiality: assurance that information is shared only among authorised persons or organisations. Breaches of

extremely harmful and dangerous types of criminal behaviour. They are classified in various ways according to the approach adopted (RAND Europe 2003).[7] There are ongoing efforts in the scientific community to create a 'common language' on computer crime. Attempts to harmonize legal definitions of computer crime are also underway in the legal community. Currently there is still no agreement on the constituent elements of computer crime as criminal offences. However, a categorization of computer crime is attempted in both the official documents considered to be the unique point of reference, especially in Europe: The Council of Europe Convention on Cybercrime[8] and the Council Framework Decision on Attacks against Information Systems presented by the European Commission.[9] They are closely connected and their definitions overlap. CIA offences are defined as follows: illegal access, illegal interception, data interference, system interference, and misuse of devices.

As regards the techniques used to commit them, they are diverse and they are used to affect hardware, software and networks. Without entering into technical details, some examples are D.o.S.,[10] homepage defacements,[11] malicious codes

---

confidentiality can occur when data is not handled in a manner adequate to safeguard the confidentiality of the information concerned. Integrity: assurance that the information is authentic and complete, so that it can be relied upon to be sufficiently accurate for its purpose. The integrity of data is not only whether the data is 'correct', but also whether it can be trusted and relied upon. Availability: assurance that the systems responsible for delivering, storing and processing information are accessible when needed, by those who need them.

Without entering into technical details, the end results of such conducts can be represented by what might be termed the 'three Ds': degradation, disruption and destruction (TRANSCRIME 2002b: 59). These three Ds are ordered on the basis of the seriousness of the damage caused to computer system and data.

7   For example, the legal approach to computer crimes is significantly different from the technical approach. In fact, legal provisions tend to be more general, in order to cover the widest set of offences and to take account of future technological innovations. Conversely, the technical perspective is extremely offence-oriented. CIA offences are mostly considered as incidents and they are studied and arranged according to the vulnerabilities exploited, the techniques and the tools used by criminals. This lack of common standards in defining computer crime inevitably impacts on the accuracy and the clarity of existing knowledge on this issue.

8   Council of Europe, Convention on Cybercrime, November 2001. The text can be retrieved from the following URL: http://conventions.coe.int/Treaty/EN/cadreprincipal.htm. Currently, the text is not legally binding. It is open for signature by C.o.E Member States and those non-Member States who participated in its elaboration. Additionally, it is open for access by other non-Member States. For the Convention to enter into force, five ratifications are necessary. This number must include at least three Member States of the Council of Europe. The status as of 11 November 2003 is as follows: total number of signatures not followed by ratifications: 34; total number of ratifications/accessions: 3.

9   Council of the European Union, Council Framework Decision on Attacks Against Information Systems, Brussels, 12 May 2003, Interinstitutional file 2002/0086 (CNS), 8687/03. The text can be retrieved from the following URL: http://register.consilium.eu.int/pdf/en/03/st08/st08687en03.pdf.

10   This is the intentional degradation or blocking of computer or network resources. It can also be distributed; attackers outside a site/network send packets of mock traffic that floods servers, preventing real users from accessing the requested information.

11   Defacements are particularly on the increase; the year 2001 saw over 20,000 cases, compared to 5,000 reported in the year 2000. This figure should not be taken lightly, considering that most of these attacks are not reported, so that there is a considerable dark number. Moreover, the number of defacements is expected to increase further in 2002.

(viruses, worms, Trojan horses, logic bombs, etc.), and hyper-worming. Some of the victims of famous D.o.S. cases are include, Yahoo.com, amazon.com, buy.com, cnn.com and eBay.com. Yahoo.com was attacked on Monday, 7 February 2000. All the others on Tuesday, 8 February 2000. Each attack lasted between one and four hours. CNN reported that the attack on its website was the first major attack it had suffered since its website went online in August1995 (Standler 2002).

The consequences of computer crime can be disastrous: this is the case, for example, of attacks against crucial private and/or public infrastructure such as air traffic control, telecommunications, power supplies or even medical and hospital services. Potentially, these attacks can cause what is called an 'electronic Pearl Harbour'.[12]

3. New technologies may be used as *tools* for the commission or planning of a crime. For example, they may be used to forge documents or to create/manipulate data and information. In these cases they constitute the instrument of the crime. This is a case which represents how technologies can also be used to commit traditional crimes, what are called *computer related crime,* or also *computer facilitated crime.* Therefore, they can be defined as traditional crimes, which can be or have been traditionally executed by other means and are now being or are capable of being executed *via* the internet, computer related venue or some other technological computing advancement (TRANSCRIME 2002b). As nearly all traditional crimes benefit from technological development, computer related crimes are by definition the largest category of misconducts. It is extremely difficult to provide a complete description of all of such activities and it is worth emphasizing that much confusion is caused by the absence of common legal definitions that can be taken as a pattern of reference. Moreover, it usually encompasses those infringements which lead only to civil sanctions. Numerous taxonomies have been developed in recent years, the aim being to categorize and order the conducts on the basis of a selected criterion. For example, types of behaviours have been divided into different classes according to the safeguarding of specific needs, such as the protection of privacy, protection against economic offences, protection of intellectual property and protection against illegal and harmful contents (Sieber 1998). In order to limit the analysis only to those behaviours that are usually prosecuted under criminal law, it is possible to organize them into three main categories. These also take into consideration the values and goods protected by the law. These are the following

---

12 Commenting about the public's awareness of the threat to America's computers from invisible attacks, Richard Clarke, the current White House 'terrorism czar' said: [CEOs of big corporations] 'think I'm talking about a 14-year-old hacking into their Web sites. I'm talking about people shutting down a city's electricity, shutting down 911 systems, shutting down telephone networks and transportation systems. You black out a city, people die. Black out lots of cities, lots of people die. It's as bad as being attacked by bombs ... Imagine a few years from now: A President goes forth and orders troops to move. The lights go out, the phones don't ring, the trains don't move. That's what we mean by an electronic Pearl Harbor' (Sussman 1999: 453).

(TRANSCRIME 2002b):
- crime against the person: any offence against the physical or psychological well-being of a person;
- crime against property: offences against public and private property;
- crime against public order and public interest: behaviours which may offend state interests or interfere with public order.

The following table reports some of the most frequent forms of harmful and criminal conduct that can be included in the above categories.

Offences against the person	Offences against property	Offences against public interest and order
Privacy infringements	Intellectual property rights infringements	Trafficking activities:
Identity theft	Fraud (some examples):	– drugs
Hate crimes	– business fraud (trading fraud, banking	– firearms
Defamation	fraud, credit card fraud, stocks	– organs
Blackmail	manipulation, etc.)	– human beings
Cyber-stalking	– investment fraud	Gambling
Prostitution	– customer fraud (online sales fraud,	Money laundering
Child exploitation	advertisement fraud, confidence tricks, etc.)	Government espionage
Child luring	Economic espionage	Corruption
Child pornography	Theft and embezzlement	Terrorism

4. In some cases, new technologies may be a *symbol* of crime. This happens, for example, when they are used to intimidate or deceive. Examples are harassment and stalking, but also some forms of sexual harassment involving minors, who are allured, and at the same time intimidated by means of internet itself.

This is the view limited to today's developments. The following paragraph will focus on cyber-offenders. It will try to understand who they are, and mainly how they use new technologies to commit unlawful behaviours.

CYBER-OFFENDERS: THE CASE OF ORGANISED GROUPS AND WHITE-COLLAR CRIMINALS

Are Criminals Really Going Cyber?

There could be different reasons to respond affirmatively to this question. What is really important to say, however, is that each human being – if suitably motivated (Felson and Clarke 1998) – could become a cyber-criminal. In fact, what has really changed, as a consequence of technological developments is the potential for crime that is offered to anyone using ICTs. This means that technologies are democratic instruments, which allow anyone to commit a crime. It does not matter who the person is, which aim s/he is seeking to achieve or what kind of crime s/he wants to perpetrate: according to his/her level of expertise and knowledge, s/he will exploit the telecommunication facilities which fit his/her purposes.

The spectrum of subjective profiles of offenders is far wider now: at one extreme of an increasing scale of potential hazard there are teenagers playing with their home computers and modems, while at the other there are ultra-dangerous and highly-skilled criminals who break into public and private networks for various purposes. In the middle there are all the people who have a suitable motivation to deliberately abuse ICTs in order to infringe civil and penal laws. This is the case of those who commit cyber-vandalism[13] and hacktivism. Particular concern is also raised by cyber-terrorists.[14] Albeit in different ways, these people are motivated by an endeavour to affirm their ideals, which may be political, social, economic and/or religious. They usually resort to violent methods in order to achieve their results and to gain visibility. They seek to demonstrate the strength and the determination of their group by focusing mass attention on their activities and mission, and they also use hacking techniques to achieve these results: examples are Web sit-ins and virtual blockades, automated e-mail bombs, web hacks, computer break-ins and computer viruses and worms.[15]

The impact of new technologies on new-generation organized criminal groups is also worrying. These are groups that use communication networks to attack information systems for their own purposes. There are organized hacking groups that are active worldwide, specializing, for example, in hacking and defacing websites. Examples include the Brazilian Silver Lords, the Pakistan Gforce and also Russian groups, which seek to extort money from their victims by offering them specialized assistance after hacking into their information systems. Similar cases have been reported in Europe. In Russia, for example, it seems that traditional criminal organizations have recruited ex-hackers and *crackerz* (through coercion or bribery or a mix of the two) to carry out computer crimes and attacks on their behalf. Recently, there have also been sophisticated, organized attacks against e-commerce sites, together with attempts to steal substantial funds from on-line banking services (Voiskounsky et al. 2000).

Numerous taxonomies of attackers and their primary motivations have been developed in the literature. They prevalently make a preliminary distinction and divide cyber-criminals into two main categories: insiders (Magklaras and Furnell 2002) and

---

13 As in the case of vandalism it is the malicious and motiveless destruction or defacement of property (Peltier 2001: 14), but it takes place by means of or against new technologies. Generally, cyber-vandalism is not an act of civil disobedience in protest against particular causes/situations. On the contrary, it is merely based on petty, personal grievances (Power 2000: 124).

14 In cyber-terrorism, there is a general progression towards greater damage and disruption, although that does not imply an increase of political effectiveness. (Denning 1999).

15 As regards virtual sit-ins and e-mail bombs, the Etoy campaign in the so-called 'Brent Spar of e-commerce' case in 1999 is a good example. Hacktivists responded to a commercial company's attempt through the courts to remove an art collective's website domain name because they found it was too similar to their own. This attack resulted in a 70% decline in the organization's NASDAQ stock value.

outsiders. Specific profiles of cyber-criminals usually encompass script-kiddies/ wannabe lamers, hackers, spies, terrorists, corporate riders, professional criminals and vandals.

Without entering into detail, attention here is focused on two specific categories of criminals: organized crime and white-collar offenders. What is interesting to know is how they are going cyber and how their criminal activities are changing due to the use of new technologies.

Certainly, they are going cyber by using ICT to communicate and collect information, because these are their primary needs. ICT helps them to substantially avoid the risk of detection. For example, new generation mobile phones allow users to encrypt their conversations in order to protect their privacy, while reducing the probability of being intercepted.[16] The list is endless: it starts with simple e-mails and continues with 'cloned' mobile phones (so called when the identity codes assigned to legitimate customers are intercepted and programmed into cellular telephones used by criminals), satellite phones, voice scramblers, etc. When calls are used with relays and interfaced with conventional landline communications, they are extremely difficult – if not almost impossible – to intercept (Rider 2001).

They are also going cyber by using ICT to better organize their activities. They can control the production of faked CDs in Macao or Hong Kong by simply sending an e-mail, and in the mean time they can verify if the ship trafficking narcotics has reached port.

As regards organized crime, new technologies are also helping criminals in other ways, which allows them to commit different crimes (Rider 2001). Money laundering, for example, is an essential 'duty' for organized groups. As already mentioned, cyber-laundering makes this a great deal easier. Internet banking facilities are perhaps the most important innovation in this sense. Indeed, profits from illegal activities can be transferred from one account to another, or loaded onto a smart card, then transferred into a computer and forwarded around the world anonymously. Drug trafficking and drug dealing can also be facilitated by ICT. At the moment, the internet trafficking of narcotic drugs and psychotropic substances does exist around the world.[17] The *Report of the International Narcotics Control Board for 2001*[18] states that drug trafficking groups utilize new technologies in two distinct ways: to improve the efficiency of product delivery and distribution through the medium of secure, instant communications; and to protect themselves and their illicit operations from investigation by drug law enforcement agencies, sometimes using counter-attack techniques. The Report explains that drug traffickers use computers and electronic pocket organizers to store information (such as bank account numbers, contact details of associates, databases of assets and financial activity, sales and other business records, grid coordinates of clandestine landing strips and recipes for synthetic drug manufacture) and for electronic mail (e-mail) and other correspondence. All these data are protected by

---

16 http://www.puntosicuro.it/language,1/page,1.php/articolo_3580/.
17 http://www.essentialdrugs.org.
18 http://www.incb.org/e/ind_ar.htm.

cryptography. Surrogates receive instructions by telephone, fax, pager or computer on where to deliver warehouse loads, whom to contact for transportation services, and where to send the profits. Greater protection derives from the use of prepaid telephone cards, broadband radio frequencies, restricted-access internet chat rooms, encryption, satellite telephony and cloned cellular telephones. Members of drug trafficking organizations can program their computers to detect attempted intrusions and to use 'back-hacking' techniques to damage the investigating source. Such techniques are of particular value to the organizers of drug trafficking activities, who rarely need to leave the protection of their home base in order to organize or supervise their operations.

The scenario will become even more sinister in the near future. For example, drug fixes could soon be paid for by cyber-payment systems. This is the case of e-cash, which allows anonymous transactions based on false or fictitious identities, which can be easily created and dissolved. Smart cards could also be useful. In fact, the micro-processor chip inserted in cyber-payment cards store a credit, which corresponds to the card's value. Blank cards can be bought in street kiosks and shops. They can also be prepaid. In all cases, they can be easily exploited for anonymous transactions, as with real cash, but can also be used to transfer and convert money.

Internet fraud will also become of interest to organized crime. In fact, it is important to stress that, although organized crime still profits from its traditional, highly lucrative activities, it is well known that it is also moving into more profitable, but less risky areas like large-scale fraud, environmental crimes, counterfeiting, piracy and the smuggling of tobacco and alcohol products (Europol 2000).

The trend towards technologies and networking has also been recorded in economic crimes. White-collar offenders are primarily interested in technological developments and the opportunities they provide for crime (Korsell 2000). Because of their status and position, they usually have access to computer data and systems, and to ICT in general.

As regards corporate crimes, for example, a first group of offences that are likely to benefit from ICTs, are those related to the falsification, alteration and suppression of data stored in computer systems. In fact, now that financial, economic and administrative information, together with communications and contacts, are mostly paperless and digitalized, they are vulnerable to a range of opportunities for crime, opportunities that could exploited either against companies, when information is counterfeited, forged and stolen by competitors, and then exploited for economic espionage, unfair competition, corruption and extortion, or by companies for committing tax evasion, financial fraud and money laundering offences.

Occupational crimes are particularly affected by ICT. In order to elaborate a general classification, crimes perpetrated by insiders can be divided into two main groups: old-style offences involving computers as a new accomplice and a second category that includes a completely new set of crimes unique to the availability and widespread use of new technologies (Doney 1998). As regards the first class of illegal conduct, crimes such as embezzlement, fraud and money laundering are, of course, not new. The *modus operandi* and the criminal techniques are, however, ever more computer-related. Other serious and common cyber-attacks carried out by disgruntled or dishonest employees include theft of proprietary information and trade secrets for sale to competitors and the sabotage of data and networks just for the sake of revenge. Some additional examples follow (Doney 1998): unauthorized use, access, modification, copying, and destruction of software, data or information; theft of money by altering computer records or theft of company/computer time; theft or destruction of hardware; use or conspiracy to use computer resources to commit a felony. As regards the impact of insider attacks, the following cases[19] show that the damage caused is not only economic. Sometimes the value of the lost or destroyed data is not even quantifiable.

In 1997, a temporary computer technician was charged with breaking into the computer system of Forbes, Inc. – publisher of Forbes magazine – causing a computer crash that cost the company more than $100,000. According to the complaint, due to the sabotage, hundreds of Forbes employees were unable to perform their server-related functions for a full day, while many employees lost a day's worth of data. In 1998, the first woman convicted for computer hacking in the United States was found guilty of trashing a U.S. Coast Guard personnel database. One of the most important cases is the Lloyd case; in May 2000, this 37-year-old former network administrator for Omega Engineering Corp. of Bridgeport (New Jersey), was convicted in the first federal prosecution of a computer sabotage case. After a three-day session, the jury stated he was guilty of planting a time bomb that deleted more than a thousand programs vital to the company's high-tech measurement and control instruments used in the manufacturing process. Lloyd had worked for Omega for 11 years. According to Omega, his sabotage resulted in damages, lost contracts, and lost productivity totalling more than $10 million.

The role of insiders should not be underestimated. Today there is no need for a disgruntled employee to carry out boxes of confidential documents and try to avoid the guards at the front gate, and competitors do not have to bribe an insider to obtain proprietary information. An unhappy or opportunistic employee can steal a company's most important trade secrets, simply by saving them onto a floppy disk and walking out the office with it in his/her pocket. Or, more easily, though at the risk of detection and sanction after the fact *via* a reconstruction by computer experts, s/he can use communication technologies, like e-mail (if not under the company's control) and instant messaging programs (when available they are still 'secure' for fraudsters because they are rarely monitored).

Moreover, as mentioned, data and information can also be stolen by gaining unauthorized access to the company's computer system. Examples abound of industrial espionage committed by *crackerz* who sell their skills and expertize in new technologies to whoever is willing to pay. It should be stressed again that these persons may be outsiders, but they could also be insiders. Besides the expertize, insiders also possess more detailed knowledge of the company, its vulnerabilities and the relative opportunities.

---

19 All the examples that follow, together with the analysis of many other cases, are reported by Power (2000: 184–185).

Besides these criminal behaviours, there is also a set of abuses and offences, which are not necessarily crime, but are nonetheless extremely serious. This is the case, for example, of internet abuses at the workplace.

THE CHALLENGES FACED BY LEGISLATION, LAW ENFORCEMENT AND SCIENCE

How Are Technologies Reshaping the Approach and the Fight against Crime at Legal, Law Enforcement and Scientific Levels?

If it is true – and it is – that ICT is impacting crime in a variety of ways, it is quite natural to wonder if it are also having the same effect on the fight against crime itself. Given that ICT is certainly bringing about dramatic changes at social, economic and organizational levels, it is likely that the response to crime is also benefiting from technological developments.

The response to crime is not only a matter of public policies, though. If considered from a wider perspective, it involves at least the law, law enforcement and also the scientific community. The needs, the problems and the expectations will be dealt with in the paragraphs below.

The Legal Response to ICT-Related Crime: Problems and Needs

As Rossi (2003) highlights,[20] economic, and financial globalisation have not been also followed by real legal globalisation. The problems are numerous and they all confirm the difficulties of penal law as an effective, efficient instrument to prevent and combat crime.

The legal framework regulating globalisation is made up of fragments at both international and national levels. At an international level there is a lack of harmonization. There are significant gaps and differences in national laws in the area of computer crime. In European law, efforts are made to regulate at least the most critical issues. As explained in the document *eEurope 2005: An Information Society for All*,[21] the European Union is trying to approach ICTs-related crime from different

---

20 'La completa e assoluta vittoria del modo di produzione capitalista nel mondo ha portato ad una globalizzazione economica, che ha raggiunto il suo apice nell'attuale fase del capitalismo finanziario, alla quale non ha però corrisposto, se non in sporadici quanto modesti tentativi, alcuna "globalizzazione giuridica" ' ['The complete and absolute victory of capitalist production methods throughout the world has led to economic globalisation, which has reached its peak in the current stage of financial capitalism, which, however, has not been reciprocated, apart from a few sporadic, modest attempts at "judicial globalisation" '].

21 Communication from the Commission to the Council, the European Parliament, the Economic and Social Committee and the Committee of the Regions, eEurope 2005: An information society for all, an Action Plan to be presented in view of the Sevilla European Council, 21/22 June 2002. This document can be retrieved from the following URL: http://www.europa.eu.int/information_society/eeurope/2002/news_library/documents/eeurope2005/eeurope2005_en.pdf.

perspectives. It has already launched a comprehensive strategy based on its Communications on Network Security,[22] cyber-crime,[23] and the current and forth-coming data protection directive regarding electronic communications. The suggested approach was endorsed and further developed by the Council Resolution of 28 January 2002 and by the recent Commission proposal for a Council Framework Decision on attacks against information systems.[24] The results are not satisfactory, however.

At a national level, the situation is no different. To date, national laws have been developed autonomously. Some countries have preferred to amend their penal/crim-inal code, while others have decided to pass specific laws on cybercrime (which were included in the penal/criminal code). There are even some countries that do not have any legal provisions regarding computer crime whatsoever.

The following table schematises the legal provisions existing in the 15 EU Member States, as regards computer crime. With the exception of Austria (that provides administrative law response) the other members states provide criminal law responses to the different violations.

Enforcing the Law: The Use of New Technologies against Crime

The difficulties encountered by law enforcement agencies when dealing with cyber-space are closely linked to the legal problems just analysed and also to the need of oper-ating in a virtual environment. In fact, legal and administrative obstacles – e.g. lack of harmonised rules, long procedural formalities, problems of jurisdiction ... – often impede police co-operation or make it extremely difficult, and slow down investigative activities. Moreover, there is lack of knowledge and training, and often law enforcement agencies are not properly equipped with advanced investigative tools and technologies.

What is interesting to analyse, however, is what can be defined as the technolo-gical paradox: law enforcement agencies exploit technologies in their crusade against crime, which – as explained – is also highly dependent on new technologies. From this standpoint, new technologies are a threat and a piece of good fortune for both criminals and law enforcement authorities. In fact, criminals enhance their activities by means of ICT, which make them vulnerable to the risks of being inter-cepted by the technological solutions used by the police, which is faced with the new challenges posed by the criminal opportunities offered by ICT. As the impact of technological developments on criminal activities has already been analysed, it is interesting to examine here how technologies are really helping law enforcement activities.

---

22 Network and Information Security: Proposal for a European Policy Approach, COM (2001) 298 of 6 June 2001.
23 Creating a Safer Information Society by improving the Security of Information Infrastructures and combating computer-related crime, COM (2000) 890 of 22 January 2001.
24 http://europa.eu.int/comm/dgs/justice_home/index_en.htm, COM (2002) 173 final of 19 April 2002.

TABLE 1. Criminality of incidents in the 15 member states of the EU.

Country	Target fingerprinting	Malicious code	Denial of service	Account compromise	Intrusion attempt	Unauthorised access to information	Unauthorised access to transmissions	Unauthorised modification of information	Unauthorised access to communication system
Austria	n.a.	n.a.	n.a.	Adm	Adm	Adm	n.a.	n.a.	Adm
Belgium	Crim	Crim	Crim	Crim	Crim	Crim	Crim	Crim	Crim
Denmark	Crim	Crim	Crim	Crim	Crim	Crim	Crim	n.a.	Crim
Finland	Crim	Crim	Crim	Crim	Crim	Crim	Crim	Crim	Crim
France	Crim	Crim	Crim	Crim	Crim	Crim	Crim	Crim	Crim
Germany	Crim	Crim	Crim	Crim	Crim	Crim	Crim	Crim	Crim
Greece	n.a.	n.a.	n.a.	Crim	Crim	Crim	n.a.	n.a.	Crim
Ireland	n.a.	n.a.	n.a.	Crim	Crim	Crim	n.a.	n.a.	Crim
Italy	Crim	Crim	Crim	Crim	Crim	Crim	Crim	Crim	Crim
Luxembourg	Crim	Crim	Crim	Crim	Crim	Crim	Crim	Crim	Crim
The Netherlands	Crim	Crim	Crim	Crim	Crim	Crim	Crim	Crim	Crim
Portugal	Crim	Crim	Crim	Crim	Crim	Crim	Crim	Crim	Crim
Spain	Crim	Crim	Crim	Crim	Crim	Crim	Crim	Crim	Crim
Sweden	Crim	Crim	Crim	Crim	Crim	Crim	Crim	Crim	Crim
United Kingdom	Crim	Crim	Crim	Crim	Crim	Crim	Crim	Crim	Crim

Source: RAND Europe (2003) and TRANSCRIME.

n.a. – no available legislation; Adm – administrative sanction provided; Crim – penal sanction provided.

Technologies are first and foremost a means of surveillance. Electronic eyes are everywhere; as Shenk (2003) emphasises, 'we are hurtling towards constant scrutiny – of the enemy and of ourselves'.

Electronic surveillance is needed to check identity. It is performed by means of surveillance cameras,[25] body scans, fingerprint and DNA databases, e-mail sifters, and phone communications interceptors. For this purpose smart cards are also used. They allow the storage of all the personal information related to the owner and also the creation a sort of national ID, which can be inserted in a central database held by the police. It is for this reason that many European countries are choosing smart cards as identity documents for their citizens.

The future of identity checks seems to rely on biometry, however.[26] The kind of data collected is of a special nature as it relates to the behavioural[27] and physiological[28] characteristics of an individual and may allow his or her unique identification. Biometric signs are mostly permanent. Previously, the use of biometrics was mainly confined to the areas of DNA and fingerprint testing. The collection of fingerprints was used in particular for law enforcement purposes (e.g. criminal investigations). Routine applications of a fingerprint or other biometric database would be risky in terms of the risk they pose to human rights and privacy infringements. Among others, future identification procedures may be carried out not only by using fingerprints, but also using irises because they are more complex, and thus leave less room for error.

Iris scans and fingerprint taking are included in the measures listed in a proposal that the Council of the European Union is going to present. The data collected will form a common European database, which is supposed to help in the fight against illegal immigration. This initiative is part of a wider reform, which will involve the entire visa system.

Identity-check systems are employed, for example, to enhance security in railway stations in the South of Italy.[29] The most innovative system is currently SPAID (*Sistema periferico di assunzione delle impronte digitali*); this is a portable system which takes a fingerprint. Portable radioscopic devices are also used to scan handbags and luggage.

---

25 As explained by Shenk (2003: 8), the UK is the most surveilled nation, with more than four million closed-circuit television cameras, including models which rotate and are equipped with wipers to clear the rain. Cameras were first installed in the 1960s.

26 Data Protection Working Party, Working document on biometrics, adopted on 1 August 2003, 12168/02/EN-WP 80.

27 It includes hand-written signature verification, keystroke analysis, gait analysis, etc.

28 Physical and physiological-based techniques measuring the physiological characteristics of a person, include: fingerprint verification, finger image, analysis, iris recognition, retina analysis, face recognition, outline of hand patterns, ear shape recognition, body odour detection, voice recognition, DNA pattern analysis and sweat pore analysis, etc.

29 'Sorveglianza nelle stazioni e più sicurezza sui treni. Dallo 'spaid' alle ispezioni non invasive dei bagagli, ecco le tecnologie per la rete ferroviaria del Mezzogiorno' ['Surveillance in stations and more security on trains. From "spaid" to the non-invasive inspection of baggage, the new technologies for the railway network of southern Italy'], in Obiettivo Sud – Newsletter mensile del Programma Operativo Nazionale 'Sicurezza per lo Sviluppo del Mezzogiorno d'Italia', December 2002, 1–2.

Electronic surveillance is crucial in preventing and deterring the commission of specific forms of crime: this is the case with violent crimes and so-called street crimes (robberies, thefts, vandalism, etc.), but also illegal immigration, for example. On the Arizona–Mexico border, motion sensors, remote-controlled cameras, night-vision apparatus and satellite control 6000 miles of border. Agents positioned on elevated platforms also use infrared cameras, which allow them to spot people two miles away, even during the night. The Italian Financial police (Guardia di Finanza), controlling the coasts of the Southern part of Italy, use special radars and night-viewers to prevent the illegal trafficking of immigrants, drugs, narcotics and cigarettes. The helicopters of the Italian Financial police, *Polizia di Stato* and *Carabinieri* are equipped with video systems that allow video recording and the transmission of images to terrestrial operations centers (Ministero degli Interni 2003). The prevention of illegal immigration is also part of the security policies of the recent Channel Tunnel, which connects France and Great Britain. The risk is that the 5000 trucks passing through it each day could also transport aliens. Cases have already occurred. Therefore, security officials are using a new technology called PMMW – passive millimetre wave imaging – which allows them to scan solid surfaces by measuring reflections of natural background radiation. After the PMMW scanner checks moving trucks looking for bodily forms, a sniffer measures the level of carbon dioxide, which is generally increased by human respiration. A similar system, called Silhouette Scan, is also used by the Italian Financial Police.

Traditional X-ray machines and metal detectors are still used, but they are less sophisticated and much more inaccurate. However, a new backscatter X-ray machine can see through a thin surface – such as truck walls – and produces images of what is behind it. It is used against illegal immigration along the Guatemala–Mexico border, where people are usually smuggled by hiding them in banana cargoes.

As regards the fight against the trafficking of drugs, narcotics, explosives and nuclear substances, Italian law enforcement agencies are using the Ionoscan 400B. This is a portable device, which very quickly detects the presence of explosives or drugs, especially cocaine, heroin, amphetamines and LSD.

Electronic surveillance is not only used against organised criminal activities. This is the case, for example, with technological instruments and devices used for traffic control and vehicle accident prevention. In Italy, the *Polizia Stradale* is equipped with a satellite system of video-surveillance, the so-called satellite access for road control (SA-RC), which has been in use since 1999.[30] Since 1998, an experiment has been underway on the highway connecting Salerno to Reggio Calabria, in the South of Italy. This portion of the highway is equipped with tele-surveillance systems, satellite control systems, and monitoring systems, which have been installed in the service areas. Sensors have been placed along the highways and mobile devices called

---

30 'Provida: il traffico si controlla a distanza. I nuovi apparecchi in dotazione alla Stradale e l'impegno per l'estate' ['Provida: remotely controlling traffic. The new equipment of the Traffic Police and the commitment for the summer'], in Obiettivo Sud – Newsletter mensile del Programma Operativo Nazionale 'Sicurezza per lo Sviluppo del Mezzogiorno d'Italia', May–June 2003, 11–13.

Provida 2000 have been installed in patrolling vehicles, which can communicate by means of a GPS system. There is also another system, called autodetector, which is used to identify vehicle number plates, and to monitor and control speed. The effects of this initiative have been notable. Crime numbers are decreasing.[31] For example, thefts have passed from 128 in 2000, to 61 in 2001. Robberies also decreased: from 31 in 2000, to 8 in 2001. People arrested were 42 in 2000, and 34 in 2001.

Electronic surveillance also lies at the basis of environmental crime prevention and trafficking in artworks. The Italian *Arma dei Carabinieri*, for example, is creating a database to store and manage information collected during monitoring activities, especially those conducted by air patrols. For this reason, helicopters are being equipped with Wescam cameras, which provide day and night vision and are also fitted with a gyroscope stabilizer.[32] These cameras can record images of distant persons, places and objects and to create a complete representation of reality, which can be sent in real time to authorities on the ground.

Electronic surveillance is also needed to intercept communications. The most criticized effort is Echelon, which can intercept and analyse computer and phone transmissions from all around the world. As Schenk (2003) emphasises, it is a clandestine ear and no one knows really why it has really been built.

Communication networks are fundamental not only for criminals, but also for law enforcement authorities. In Italy, a digital inter-force radio link is under construction and will connect all the police offices in the South of Italy. This will reduce telecommunication costs, and increase co-operation and synergy (Ministero degli Interni 2003).

A centralized database, which will serve all European law enforcement agencies, is also under construction.[33] It will be used in the fight against organized crime and terrorism, because it will enhance co-operation and communications between the police forces of different countries.

This scenario raises some thoughts and questions, though. As we have seen, electronic surveillance is needed to enhance security, but it is pervasive in modern societies. In conclusion, some questions are as follows: Is there a trade-off between security and privacy? Are people really aware of the level of electronic surveillance and control they are under? Are technologies really needed to prevent and combat crime? How much do institutions and law enforcement agencies invest in technologies against crime? And what about the legal framework regulating electronic surveillance: is it capable of balancing individual rights with security and crime prevention needs?

---

31 'Operazione autostrade. Potenziata la telesorveglianza nel Sud' ['Operation motorway. The expansion of remote surveillance in the South'], in Obiettivo Sud – Newsletter mensile del Programma Operativo Nazionale 'Sicurezza per lo Sviluppo del Mezzogiorno d'Italia', December 2002, 4.

32 'Wescam: ambiente sotto osservazione' ['Wescam: the environment under observation'], in Obiettivo Sud – Newsletter mensile del Programma Operativo Nazionale 'Sicurezza per lo Sviluppo del Mezzogiorno d'Italia', May–June 2003, 12.

33 'Banche dati in comune tra le polizie europee' ['Common databases for European police forces'], in *La Repubblica*, 7 October 2003, 16.

The Role of the Scientific Community: The Need for Knowledge,
Training and Co-operation

There is a strong demand for knowledge and support, coming from the public and the private sectors, which is addressed to the scientific community. This aspect is crucial and requires the attention of the entire scientific community. Technology-related disciplines, human and social sciences (criminology, but also sociology and psychology *in primis*), law and economics are involved.

This means that there is urgent need for research and studies, for training and co-operation in the field of crime analysis and prevention. This is a problem for both public and private security. In fact, public institutions, law enforcement agencies and also private companies, do not have the prerequisites nor the structures to develop complete, integrated knowledge-based solutions. From this standpoint, information sharing is essential.

As regards the development of research and studies, applications for risk analysis, vulnerabilities and risk assessment studies are particularly needed. Further research should also be oriented towards the development of crime-proofing mechanisms. Crime proofing is a new methodology, which allows the outlining, analysing and evaluation of the *criminogenicity* of both laws and products. Legal rules can produce both criminal opportunities for crime, and products as well. These opportunities may be caused as direct or indirect effects. In short, the aim of this methodology is to reduce crime risks by means of the quantification and reduction of criminal opportunities.

As far as ICT-related crime is concerned, greater attention to methodology and scientific approach is also required. This is particularly true when analysing the subjective profiles of attackers. The rapid escalation of technology-related crimes has inevitably led to the drafting of a range of studies of the profiles of the authors and their motivations. However, several difficulties have been encountered in compiling such profiles. It is not easy to point out a criterion with which to classify classification systems because each individual may potentially be a criminal. From the analytical perspective, this implies that additional efforts have to be made to systematize subjective profiles into well-ordered categories. Currently it is difficult to trust existing profiles, which are really proliferating. In most cases, for example, it is not possible to verify the methodology used and/or the sources of information. Often, there is a sort of abuse of false myths – which prevalently belong to the mass media representation of technology-related crime and attackers – which results in nothing but a useless and risky misrepresentation of reality. In fact, these mythical, fabled descriptions of the hacker's way of life make people perceive them as fascinating anti-heroes whom they can emulate. This highlights the need for a scientific approach to this issue.[34]

---

34 One of the most important – even if controversial – efforts in this sense is the Honeynet Project (http://www.honeynet.org). This American initiative begins with the following premise: how is it possible to defend against an enemy, when there is no knowledge about who the enemy is? This stated,

Coming back to the role of the scientific community, and to the need for information sharing, the scientific community is asked to promote and organize training activities for law enforcement personnel, prosecutors and judges in order to improve their knowledge of high-tech crimes and the use of technologies to combat unlawful and illegal behaviour. It is also asked to improve co-operation and reinforce partnerships, in order to outline new *fora*, where important issues can be addressed, discussed and developed. The scientific community, and especially Universities, should also design new curricula for training students, who need to acquire better knowledge about high-tech-crime and its civil and criminal legal implications or about the use of technologies to combat crime. In general, the scientific community is expected to play an active role in contributing to understanding the new reality with which modern societies are experimenting. It is asked to analyse and explain both sides of the situation: the physiological and natural changes that are development, and also its negative and pathological implications, which is crime.

REFERENCES

Adamoli, S., A. Di Nicola, E. U. Savona and P. Zoffi, Organised crime around the world. Helsinki: HEUNI Publication Series No. 31, 1998.
Akdeniz, Y., Controlling illegal and harmful content on the Internet. In: D. Wall (Ed.), *Crime and the Internet*, pp. 113–140. London: Routledge, 2001.
Beck, U., *World Risk Society*. Cambridge: Polity Press, 1999.

---

the project aims at learning the tools, the tactics, and the motives of the blackhat community, and at sharing the lessons learned. The initiators are volunteer security professionals researching cyber threats, who have three main goals: to raise awareness of the threats that exist, for those already aware, to teach and inform about the threats, and to give organizations the capabilities to learn more on their own. The group informally began its activities in April, 1999 as the Wargames mail-list. It officially decided to call itself the Honeynet Project in June 2000, and formed the Honeynet Research Alliance in January 2002. The Alliance is an international initiative involving the following members: South Florida Honeynet Project, Georgia Technical Institute, Azusa Pacific University, Paladion Networks Honeynet Project (India), Internet Systematics Lab Honeynet Project (Greece), Mexico Honeynet (Mexico), Honeynet.BR (Brazil), Irish Honeynet, Norwegian Honeynet, UK Honeynet, French Honeynet Project, Italian Honeynet Project (http://www.iritaly.org). Information is collected by means of the so-called honeypot, which is an information system resource whose value lies in unauthorized or illicit use of that resource. This information system is somewhat fictitious, in the sense that it has no production value. Examples of the advantages are that honeypots allow the collection of small high value data sets, reduce false positives, catch new attacks, false negatives, while requiring minimal resources. The most relevant disadvantage is represented by the fact that a honeypot only allows a limited field of view, as it is a microcosm. In order to limit this specific disadvantage, honeynets were created. Honeynets are an architecture made up of live systems, which presents a high level of interaction and is designed to capture in-depth information. Every packet entering or leaving is monitored, captured, and analysed. Thus, information collected is not theoretical, but totally empirical. There are also risks that need to be taken into consideration. First, honeynets are highly complex, and require extensive resources and manpower to maintain properly. They are also a high-risk technology. In fact, they can be used to attack or harm other non-honeynet systems. From a legal standpoint, honeypots and honeynets also pose some issues. For example, there are implications in terms of privacy and liability.

Becker, G.S., Crime and punishment: An economic approach. In: G. Becker and W. Landes (Eds.), *Essays in the Economic of Crime and Punishment*, pp. 1–54. New York: Columbia University Press, 1974.

Brill, A., Cyberlaundering: The American experience: Presentation and analysis of specific cases in the USA. Paper presented at the workshop Cyberlaundering 2000. *The Risk of Money Laundering via Internet*, organised by TRANSCRIME-University of Trento, Trento, Italy, 11 June 1999.

Cornish, D.B. and R.V.G. Clarke, *The Reasoning Criminal: Rational Choice Perspectives on Offending*. New York: Springer-Verlag, 1986.

Denning, D., *Information Warfare and Security*. Essex: Addison Wesley, 1999.

Doney, L., The growing threat of computer crime in small business, *Business Horizons*, May–June 1998.

Europol 2000. *EU Organised Crime Situation Report*. The Hague: Europol.

Felson, M. and R.V.G. Clarke, Opportunity makes the thief: Practical theory for crime prevention. Police Research Series-Paper 98, London: Home Office, 1998.

Forte, D., International hacking: When the cooperation is the only cure. Paper presented at the Black Hat USA 2003 Convention, Washington, 23 October 2003. Retrieved from http://www.blackhat.com/presentations/bh-usa-03/bh-us-03-forte.ppt, 2003.

International Narcotics Control Board. *Report of the International Narcotics Control Board for 2001*. Retrieved from http://www.incb.org/e/ind_ar.htm, 2001.

Korsell, L.E., *Information Technology and Economic Crime – Old Wine in New Bottles or a Threat to the New Millennium*. National Council for Crime Prevention-Sweden, 2000.

Magklaras, G.B. and S.M. Furnell, Insider threat prediction tool: Evaluating the probability of IT misuse. *Computers & Security*, 21(1), pp. 62–73, 2002.

Malagò, T. and M. Mignone, *Crimini and musica on line. Gli sviluppi della pirateria musicale attraverso le nuove tecnologie: Analisi e rimedi*. Milan: FrancoAngeli Editore, 2000.

Ministero degli Interni. Il programma operativo nazionale per il Mezzogiorno – sicurezza per lo sviluppo del Mezzogiorno d'Italia. In: *Rapporto sulla Sicurezza*, 2003.

Ogilvie, E., Cyberstalking. *Trends and Issues in Crime and Criminal Justice*, 166. Australian Institute of Criminology, 2000.

Peltier, T.R., *Information Security Risk Analysis*. Boca Raton: Auerbach, 2001.

Power, R., *Tangled Web: Tales of Digital Crime from the Shadows of Cyberspace*. Indianapolis: Que Corporation, 2000.

RAND Europe. *Handbook of Legislative Procedures of Computer and Network Misuse in EU Countries*. Study for the European Commission Directorate-General Information Society, 2003.

Rider, B., Cyber-organised crime: The impact of information technology on organized crime. *Journal of Financial Crime*, 8(4), pp. 332–346, 2001.

Shenk, D., Watching you: The world of high-tech surveillance. *National Geographic*, November pp. 2–29, 2003.

Sieber, U., *The Legal Aspect of Computer Related Crime in the Information Society*. COMCRIME Study, 1998.

Standler, R.B., *Computer crime*. Retrieved from http://www.rbs2.com/ccrime.htm, 2002.

The Honeynet Project 2002. *Know Your Enemy: Revealing the Security Tools, Tactics, and Motives of the Blackhat Community*. Essex: Addison Wesley.

Thomas, D. and B.D. Loader, Introduction. In: D. Thomas and B.D. Loader (Eds), *Cybercrime: Law Enforcement, Security and Surveillance in the Information Age*. London: Routledge, 2000.

TRANSCRIME. *Business Crime Prevention in Europe: Implementing an Early Warning Strategy. Final Report*. Study financed by the European Commission under the 2001 Falcone Programme, 2002a.

TRANSCRIME. *Transatlantic Agenda. EU/US Co-operation for Preventing Computer Related Crime. Final Report.* Study financed by the European Commission under the Transatlantic Agenda Programme, 2002b.

Voiskounsky, A.E., J.D. Babaeva and O.V. Smyslova, Attitudes towards computer hacking in Russia. In: D. Thomas and B.D. Loader (Eds), *Cybercrime, Law Enforcement, Security and Surveillance in the Information Age.* London: Routledge, 2000.

CHAPTER 3

NEW CHALLENGES FOR INTERNATIONAL RULES AGAINST CYBER-CRIME*

Fausto Pocar

INTRODUCTION

In light of current approaches adopted by international institutions dealing with cyber-crime and existing legal instruments in this area, this paper aims at identifying the main issues which require further consideration for the purposes of combating this criminal phenomenon. Such issues include the definition of crimes and of sanctions, an enhanced international cooperation between domestic authorities, and harmonized criteria for establishing jurisdiction over cyber-crimes.

THE NEED FOR INTERNATIONAL INSTRUMENTS

It is almost banal to remark that crime follows human technological progress: as cyber-space was established as a new medium of communication, criminal activity followed in parallel. In addition, this kind of criminal activity takes advantage of and expands as a result of all the opportunities offered by the internet, i.e. the evolution of e-commerce, the growth of multinational companies, the ease and speed with which information can be passed around the world, the security and anonymity provided by this technology, and, above all, the territorial dimension of traditional legal approaches. Finally, for organized crime "[t]he spoils (...) are significant and the risk must appear very low" (National Hi-Tech Crime Unit 2002)[1] and this situation leads to great vulnerability for any member of the international community.

This chapter was previously published in *European Journal on Criminal Policy and Research* **10**: 39–53, 2004.

* The substance of this article reflects a paper submitted by the author to the International Conference on *Crime and Technology: New Frontiers for Legislation, Law Enforcement and Research,* held in Courmayeur (Italy) on 28–30 November 2003.

1 The National Hi-Tech Crime Unit (NHTCU) is part of the United Kingdom's National Hi-Tech Crime Strategy (NHTCS), founded in April 2002, based in London, whose role is defined as follows: supporting and leading activity against serious and organized hi-tech crime of a national and transnational nature; responding with an investigative capability to all threats to and attacks upon the critical

Ernesto U. Savona (ed.), Crime and Technology: New Frontiers for Regulations, Law Enforcement and Research, 29–38.
© 2004 *Springer. Printed in The Netherlands.*

A recent *Proposal of the Commission of the European Union for a Council Framework Decision on Attacks against Information Systems*[2] organizes in these terms the phenomenon: "Computer-related crimes are committed across cyberspace and do not stop at the conventional, political state-borders. They can, in principle, be perpetrated from anywhere and against any computer user in the world. (...) Given the worldwide dimension of the internet, safety and confidence in cyber – space is an activity which calls for a collective response on a global scale. (...)".[3] The dichotomy is, indeed, between the globalization of crime and the territoriality of domestic law, generally confined to a specific territory.

Thus, "solutions to the problems posed must be addressed by international law, necessitating the adoption of adequate international legal instruments", including, in particular, "binding international instruments, that can ensure the necessary efficiency in the fight against these new phenomena" (Council of Europe 2001b).

INTERNATIONAL LEGAL SOURCES ON CYBER-CRIME

In order to identify the issues that combating cyber-crime may raise, it is important to briefly describe the relevant international legal sources and instruments that have been elaborated on the matter so far. They relate to different levels of cooperation, at both the universal and regional level.

At the universal level, the United Nations has been called upon to play an important role. This organization works through its policy-making body (developing relevant recommendations[4]) and its many agencies, such as the Commission on Crime Prevention and Criminal Justice (within the Economic and Social Council) or the Office of Drug Control and Crime Prevention: the first agency adopted a *Plan of Action* dealing with the prevention and control of high-technology and computer-related crimes (UN Economic and Social Council 2001); the second is carrying out this plan.

Notwithstanding that not all transnational computer crimes belong to the area of "organized crime", attention should also be given to the *Palermo Convention against Transnational Organized Crime* (signed on 15 December 2000),[5] the purpose of which

---

national infrastructure; undertaking strategic threat assessments; developing intelligence; supporting and coordinating law enforcement operations; offering 'best advice' to other law enforcement agencies, business, industry and the IT world.

2 Commission of the European Union, Proposal for a Council Framework Decision on Attacks against Information Systems, in *Official Journal of European Communities*, C 203 E, 27 August 2002, pp. 109–113.

3 *Ibidem.*

4 See, in particular, General Assembly resolutions 56/121 of 19 December 2001 and 56/261 of 31 January 2002: in the first resolution the General Assembly underlines the need for enhanced cooperation among states in combating the criminal misuse of information technologies and stresses the role that could be played by the United Nations and the other universal and regional international Organizations; in the second one the General Assembly took note of the UN Plan of Action (UN Economic and Social Council, 2001) and invited member states and the Secretary-General to consider the formulation of legislation policies and programmes on the matter.

5 The text of the convention is available at http://www.odccp.org/palermo.

is the "prevention, investigation and prosecution" of this kind of criminality. The latter comprises enumerated crimes (arts. 5, 6, 8 and 23), as well as crimes referred to simply as "serious crimes", each "conduct constituting an offence punishable by a maximum deprivation of liberty of at least four years or a more serious penalty".[6]

The United Nations is not alone in approaching the issues raised by cyber-crime; other entities are actively working on this topic from different perspectives. One could mention the OECD (Organization for Economic Cooperation and Development), whose effort is directed towards establishing transparent relationships inside private sector companies, in order to ensure free competition. In this perspective the Organization adopted the *Guidelines on the Security of Information Systems and Networks* (OECD 2002),[7] that call for the development of a 'culture of security', to ensure the stable evolution of the digital economy and information society.[8]

On a different level, one also has to consider the activity of non-governmental entities, such as the International Association for Criminal Law, whose resolutions and recommendations may guide policy-making authorities.[9]

Among regional organizations, the activity of the Council of Europe and the European Union is particularly relevant.

The first circle of cooperation has led to the adoption of the *Convention on Cyber-Crime* (Council of Europe 2001a)[10] and its *Additional Protocol* (Council of Europe 2003). The Council of Europe Convention is the first multilateral treaty on cyber-crime. It provides the basic framework for the establishment by contracting states of domestic substantive and procedural laws aimed at combating all types of computer-related crimes, and the means whereby states can cooperate expeditiously with one another during the course of transnational investigations. Its protocol is devoted to combating acts of a racist and xenophobic nature committed through computer systems.

As regards the second circle, the acts adopted within the framework of the so-called third pillar of the European Union (arts 29ff. of the EU Treaty) should be mentioned. For the time being, the efforts against cyber-crimes are spelled out in the above-mentioned *Proposal of the Commission of the European Union for a Council Framework Decision on Attacks against Information Systems*, in the *Council Decision*

---

6   Art. 2, letter b) of the Palermo Convention.
7   So called '2002 Security Guidelines', available at http://www.oecd.org/dataoecd/59/0/1946946.pdf.
8   OECD also discussed the principles contained in the first edition of a *Global Action Plan for Electronic Commerce*, prepared by the Alliance for Global Business in October 1998, which urged governments to rely on business self-regulation and the voluntary use of empowering technologies as the main drivers, behind the creation of trust across the whole spectrum of users and providers of e-commerce goods and services; it also stated that governments should focus on the provision of a stable, predictable environment enabling the enforcement of electronic contracts, the protection of intellectual property and safeguarding competition. The second edition of this plan (Alliance for Global Business, 1999) establishes a set of fundamental principles as the basis for the framework in which policymaking for electronic commerce should take place.
9   As to cyber-criminality see, for example, the resolutions and recommendations adopted at the meeting of the International Association for Criminal Law held on 28 October 2002 (resolutions and recommendations are available at http://www.penal.org).
10 The Convention was signed in Budapest on 23 November 2001.

of 29 May 2000 to Combat Child Pornography on the internet,[11] in the *Proposal for a Regulation of the European Parliament and of the Council Establishing the European Network and Information Security Agency,*[12] in the *Council Recommendation of 25 June 2001 on Contact Points Maintaining a 24-Hour Service for Combating High-Tech Crime,*[13] as well as and in the *Common Position of 27 May 1999 adopted by the Council on the basis of Article 34 of the Treaty on European Union, on Negotiations Relating to the Draft Convention on Cyber Crime held in the Council of Europe*[14] and in the *Joint Position of 29 March 1999 defined by the Council on the basis of Article K.3 of the Treaty on European Union, on the proposed United Nations Convention against Organised Crime.*[15] The European Commission has also been active in the debate with its *Communication on Creating a Safer Information Society by Improving the Security of Information Infrastructures and Combating Computer related-Crime.*[16]

In the European context, it should also be noted that the EU member states have ratified the *EUROPOL Convention,*[17] which provides for a framework of police cooperation against organized crimes, thus also involving cyber-criminality.

In light of the foregoing indications, it appears that the list of international legal instruments dealing with cyber-crime is rather long. However, it is far from exhaustive for the purposes of covering all aspects of the subject matter concerned. Moreover, it should be noted that, apart from EU legislation, not one of the mentioned legally binding international instruments is yet in force. In general terms, existing international rules have been structured along two different though compatible routes. On the one hand, they provide for the duty of contracting states to implement internationally agreed norms within their own borders, with a view to bringing the legal system of contracting states closer both as to the substance and the practice of criminal law.

---

11 Council of the European Union, Council Decision of 29 May 2000 to Combat Child Pornography on the internet, in *Official Journal of the European Communities,* L 138, 9 June 2000, pp. 1–4.

12 Commission of the European Union, Proposal for a Regulation of the European Parliament and of the Council Establishing the European Network and Information Security Agency, 11 February 2003, COM (2003) 63 final.

13 Council of the European Union, Council Recommendation of 25 June 2001 on Contact Points Maintaining a 24-Hour Service for Combating Hi-Tech Crime, in *Official Journal of European Communities,* C 187, 3 July 2001, pp. 5–6.

14 Council of the European Union, Common Position of 27 May 1999 adopted by the Council on the basis of Article 34 of the Treaty on European Union, on Negotiations Relating to the Draft Convention on Cyber Crime held in the Council of Europe, in *Official Journal of the European Communities,* L 142, 5 June 1999, pp. 1–2.

15 Council of the European Union, Joint Position of 29 March 1999 defined by the Council on the basis of Article K.3 of the Treaty on European Union, on the proposed United Nations Convention against Organised Crime, in *Official Journal of the European Communities,* L 87, 31 March 1999, pp. 1–2.

16 Commission of the European Union, Communication from the Commission to the Council, the European Parliament, the Economic and Social Committee and the Committee of the Regions on 'Creating a Safer Information Society by Improving the Security of Information Infrastructures and Combating Computer-related Crime', 26 January 2001.

17 Council of the European, Council Act of 26 July 1995 drawing up the Convention based on Article K.3 of the Treaty on European Union, on the establishment of a European Police Office (Europol Convention), in *Official Journal of the European Communities,* C 316, 27 November 1995, p. 1.

On the other hand, these rules establish procedures for relevant international relations, aimed at providing such forms of cooperation between national judicial authorities as may interact with each other both swiftly and efficiently.[18]

DEFINING CYBER-CRIMES IN INTERNATIONAL LEGISLATION

Among the various issues that may arise from existing international legislation on cyber-crime and efforts aimed at establishing new legal instruments, two appear to be especially sensitive: the definition of cyber-crimes and the sanctions to be applied to perpetrators.

The first issue concerns an aspect which may at first sight appear to be of a purely terminological nature, i.e., the definition of the activities included in the expression 'cyber-crime'. It is, however, a very substantive issue, both because it deals with the problem of identifying the elements of cyber-crime, which is a central prerequisite for criminal prosecution, and because of its impact on the effectiveness of international cooperation in the field. The problems that arise in this context may be summarized as follows.

First, the terms 'cyber-crime', 'computer crime', 'computer-related crime' and 'high-tech(nology) crime' are often used interchangeably, without an appreciation of different substantive grounds. However, these terms cover different crimes. By way of example, Europol assumed that 'high technology crime' consists of the use of information and telecommunications technology to commit or further a criminal act, against a person, property, organization or the network computer system. 'Cyber-crime' (and its sub-categories) is the criminal use of any computer network or system on the internet; attacks or abuse against the systems and networks for criminal purposes; crimes and abuse from either existing criminals using new technology; or new crimes that have developed with the growth of the internet.

Secondly, this terminological confusion exists in addition to diverging international praxis and domestic laws: different views exist on what constitutes crime involving the internet in some way. In other words, national legal orders have different approaches to this phenomenon (Podgor 2002).

A common aspect is represented by the *noyau dur* of six kinds of behaviours, viz., intellectual property theft or software piracy, hacking and virus attacks, organized on-line paedophilia, denial of service attacks, extortion, and fraud. As one can see, some of these crimes may also be perpetrated outside the internet. And indeed, almost any crime that can be committed in the real world can also be perpetrated in the virtual one; but it is beyond doubt that some crimes have been revitalized as a result of the electronic environment.

This situation entails the need for clarification at the legal level, based on a consideration of distinct factual situations: a computer may be the 'object' of the crime (because it is targeted), the 'subject' (as it is the physical site of the crime), or the 'source' (as viruses and worms start from it).

---

18   In a similar vein, as regards international legal efforts on combating corruption, see Parisi and Rinoldi (2004).

It follows that a comprehensive definition could only be very general, such as defining cyber-crime as the criminal use of any computer network or system on the internet, which implies attacks on or abuse of the system and network for criminal purposes.

Scholars also distinguish between 'vertical' computer crimes and 'horizontal' ones (i.e. computer-related crimes) (Clarberg 2003, p. 2). This partition is also followed in the solution offered by existing international rules as well as by some international instruments in the course of their adoption, which appear to distinguish between 'computer specific crimes' and 'traditional crimes performed with the aid of computer technology'. Such is the case of the Council of Europe *Convention on Cyber-Crime*,[19] and its *Additional Protocol*,[20] as well as of the mentioned *Proposal for a Council Framework Decision on Attacks against Information Systems*.

In this context, international legal instruments should be aimed at harmonizing the material elements of crime envisaged by domestic legislations, with a view to establishing a common international *minimum standard* of relevant offences that is internationally imposed. It is self-evident that this task also entails a revision of substantive laws in many areas of national legislation, such as the legal data protection regime (and privacy), electronic surveillance, abilities to secure traffic data, and others. Unfortunately, existing legal instruments currently leave a precise description of cyber-crimes to domestic legislation, and this may entail major difficulties in their effective application when they come into force, unless parallel harmonization efforts are successful.

A second delicate area is undoubtedly the sanctions area. Two different issues may be identified as emerging from existing legal instruments or proposals. The first one relates to the type of sanctions that should be imposed on perpetrators. Following a well-founded practice, international legal instruments oblige contracting/member states to establish sanctions that are "effective, proportionate and dissuasive". The Budapest Convention contains provisions in these terms (art. 13); the same applies to the European Union *Proposal for a Council Framework Decision on Attacks against Information Systems*. However, the nature (criminal, administrative or civil) of the sanctions tends to be left to each state, as pertaining to its domestic jurisdiction.[21] Here too, as in the area of definition of crimes, serious difficulties may arise in coordinating activities intended to combat cyber-crimes, unless efforts aiming at harmonizing national legislation are not only encouraged, but successfully carried out, in order that sanctions may constitute an effective deterrent against the commission of violations in this field. The second issue relates to the need to establish criminal liability also for legal persons, and to provide the possibility of imposing monetary sanctions on them, following a route indicated by the *OECD 1997 Convention on Combating Bribery of Foreign Officials in International Business Transactions* (OECD 1997).[22]

---

19   Arts 2–13.
20   Arts 3–7.
21   Following the teaching of the Court of Justice of the European Communities in the so-called 'mais case' (judgement 21 September 1989, case No. 68/88).
22   The Convention came into force internationally on 15 February 1999.

ENHANCING INTERNATIONAL COOPERATION ON COMBATING CYBER-CRIMES

The abovementioned difficulties show that international legislation and efforts aimed at the harmonization of national laws and procedures would be almost bound to miss the mark if they are not accompanied by effective international cooperation: the world-wide dimension of the internet implies that its illegal use and related offences must prompt responses and concerted efforts from all relevant domestic and international authorities.

In this context, mutual cooperation among domestic judicial authorities plays a critical role. Such cooperation is mainly based, in traditional legal instruments concerned with combating serious crimes, on the principle *aut dedere aut judicare*. The same approach also tends to be followed as far as cyber-crime is concerned.

In this scenario the principle may undergo new developments, at least at the European level, from the adoption of the European arrest warrant,[23] which involves a form of handing over the suspect person based on the recognition – by the judicial authorities of the requested state – of the restrictions on personal freedom (albeit not definitive) adopted by the judicial authorities of another member state. The mutual trust in the system of administration of criminal justice allows the transfer to take place in the absence of the traditional evaluation of political considerations by non-judicial authorities, as in the case of extradition. Furthermore, the warrant excludes the need to respect the criterion of double jeopardy, thus minimizing the impact of differences in the domestic legislation of member states. Whether a system of this kind, based on the principle of mutual recognition, may be exported to other countries is hard to say, in light of the difficulties that its establishment is encountering in the European Union itself. However, there is no doubt that the form of cooperation that it implies would contribute substantially to fighting such crimes as cyber-crimes, which are international in nature (Parisi and Rinoldi 2004).

In any event, and apart from this scenario, it has to be stressed that almost all different forms of mutual cooperation presuppose the respect of the dual criminality criterion. But, in turn, the application of the latter requires a harmonized approach to the definition of the crimes involved. An efficient cooperation in the implementation of the principle *aut dedere aut judicare* is therefore strictly linked to successful efforts in bringing domestic legislations on cyber-crime closer.

INVESTIGATION AND PROSECUTION OF CYBER-CRIMES

From another point of view, international mutual cooperation is also necessary for investigation and prosecution purposes. Indeed, combating offences such as those under consideration requires strategic intelligence on hi-tech criminality, tactical

---

23 Council of the European Union, Framework Decision of 13 June 2002 on the European Arrest Warrant and the Surrender Procedures between Member States, in *Official Journal of the European Communities,* L 190, 18 July 2002, pp. 1–20.

intelligence aimed at identifying new hi-tech criminality targets for investigation, and intelligence support to the operational activities of international agencies, such as Interpol and Europol.

One has to wonder whether traditional procedural measures (such as search and seizure) are also useful in the new technological environment, or whether new measures should be envisaged. One could think, for example, of expediting the preservation of data, in order to ensure that traditional measures of collection remain effective in the volatile technological area; or developing and implementing a tactical hi-tech crime intelligence database and a confidential source register, which would allow for the protection of the identity of sources of information, following the example of national agencies such as the British National Hi-Tech Crime Unit. In this context, one could mention that the European Union is adopting a very interesting *Framework Decision on the European Evidence Warrant for Obtaining Objects, Documents and Data for Use in Proceedings in Criminal Matters.*[24]

Finally, one has to stress that interstate cooperation may not be sufficient to cover all aspects of cyber-crime. High priority should also be given to enhancing cooperation between public authorities and private companies involved in the production and commerce of hardware and software, as well as of those involved in the delivery of services in the area. Strategic and closer relationships could help both the policy and legislative level and the investigative and law enforcement level, in particular as far as some types of cyber-crimes (such as online fraud, hackers and virus writers) are involved (UN Economic and Social Council 2002).

SOME REMARKS ON JURISDICTION OVER CYBER-CRIMES

Prosecuting and trying persons allegedly responsible for cyber-crimes also raises difficult problems in the field of jurisdiction. These problems relate to the determination of the place where the offence was committed (*locus delicti*), to the application of *ne bis in idem* principle when several jurisdictions are equally competent, and to the avoidance of negative jurisdiction conflicts.

It is well known that the existence of various principles to ground domestic criminal jurisdiction is generally recognized and that jurisdictional problems are not new in the practice of international relations (Jennings and Watts 1992, pp. 137–139). The principles on which criminal jurisdiction is normally based in domestic legislation are the *territoriality* principle, whereby an alleged perpetrator can be brought before the courts of the state where the crime was committed, and the *nationality* principle, whereby the courts of a state have jurisdiction to try a national of that state, irrespective of the place where the crime was committed. The nationality principle is also frequently invoked in order to attribute jurisdiction to the courts of a state over

---

24 Commission of the European Union, Proposal for a Council Framework Decision on the European Evidence Warrant for Obtaining Objects, Documents and Data for Use in Proceedings in Criminal Matters, 14 November 2003, COM (2003) 688 final.

a foreigner when the victim of the crime is a national of that state, irrespective, again, of the place where the criminal activity was performed.

It has to be stressed, however, that the territoriality principle may appear to be of limited value when cyber-crimes are at issue, in light of the borderless nature of the internet. However, legal practice appears to accept it, coupled with the principle of nationality, which may be more suitable in several cases, especially if it were to be used in relation to victims of cyber-crimes, since it would at least enable a state to protect its nationals, if not all the victims of the crimes.

Finally, one could mention in this context the principle of *universality* as a ground for criminal jurisdiction. Normally, this principle has been invoked as applicable to the exercise of jurisdiction over a narrow range of crimes (none of them typically computer-related), such as crimes against humanity, war crimes, and genocide. It has also received some recognition in a few treaties aimed at combating other crimes that the international community regards as crimes of an international nature, such as air-craft hijacking.[25] In light of the borderless character of cyber-space, one may wonder whether universal jurisdiction, accompanied by an obligation to follow the principle *aut dedere aut judicare,* would provide an interesting.approach for the resolution of jurisdictional issues in this area, which merits careful consideration.

It appears, on the contrary, that international courts and tribunals would hardly have a role to play in this field, unless specific cyber-crimes result in serious viola-tions of human rights, which would be regarded as crimes against humanity. Only such a case would justify the intervention of international jurisdiction to try cases which would not be brought before domestic courts, due to the inability or the unwill-ingness of states to do so.

REFERENCES

Alliance for Global Business, *A Global Action Plan for Electronic Commerce,* 2nd ed., October, 1999.

Clarberg, B., *Cyber Crime,* Paper presented at the conference on *International Cooperation on Trans-National Crime,* The Hague, 9–10 October, 2003 (unpublished).

Council of Europe, *Convention on Cyber-Crime.* Budapest, 23 November 2001a.

Council of Europe, *Convention on Cyber-Crime, Explanatory Report.* 8 November 2001b.

Council of Europe, *Additional Protocol to the Convention on Cyber-Crime Concerning the Criminalisation of Acts of a Racist and Xenophobic Nature Committed through Computer Systems.* Strasbourg, 28 January 2003.

Jennings, R. and A. Watts (Eds.), *Oppenheim's International Law,* 9th ed., London: Longman, 1992.

---

25 As of the Tokyo Convention on Offences and Certain Other Acts Committed on Board Aircraft, 1963, which was followed by the Hague Convention for the Suppression of Unlawful Seizure of Aircraft, 1970, and by the Montreal Convention for the Suppression of Unlawful Acts against the Safety of Civil Aviation, 1971. For a consideration of these and other conventions that adopt the principle of universal jurisdiction, see e.g. Shaw (1997: p. 470 ff).

National Hi-Tech Crime Unit, *Operational Protocol between the National Hi-Tech Crime Unit and Parties within the Strategic Stakeholders.* May, 2002.

OECD, *Convention on Combating Bribery of Foreign Officials in International Business Transactions.* 21 November, 1997.

OECD, *OECD Guidelines for the Security of Information Systems and Networks. Towards a Culture of Security.* Paris: OECD, 2002.

Parisi, N. and D. Rinoldi, Recent Evolutions in the Fight against Corruption in the International Trade Law, *Le droit des affaires internationales,* p. 1, 2004.

Podgor, E.S. International computer fraud: A paradigm for limiting national jurisdiction, *U.C. Davis Law Review,* p. 35, 2002.

Shaw, M., *International Law,* 4th ed., New York: Cambridge University Press, 1997.

UN Economic and Social Council, *Official Records of the Economic and Social Council, 2001, Supplement No. 10 (E/2001/30/Rev.1),* 2001.

UN Economic and Social Council, *Effective Measures to Prevent and Control Computer-Related Crime. Report of the Secretary-General.* 29 January, 2002.

CHAPTER 4

COMBATING CYBER-CRIME: NATIONAL LEGISLATION AS A PRE-REQUISITE TO INTERNATIONAL COOPERATION

Lucie Angers[1]

INTRODUCTION

Nothing has more revolutionized and shrunk the world we live in than the internet. This network of networks of computers, initially intended for communication between an elite working on military issues, has become one of the most common environments in which we do business, entertain ourselves and work. No more do we call our colleagues to invite them for lunch; we send them an e-mail instead. Doctors in one country can make a diagnosis of a disease affecting a person thousands of miles away. We purchase goods through the internet, we make friends over the internet and we access huge amounts of information on the internet. The internet is at the heart of a considerable part of our busy days.

The purpose of this paper was initially to deal with international cooperation in combating computer and computer related crime or as it is more commonly known today, cyber-crime. However, it is impossible to address the issue of international cooperation without first dealing with two of its pre-requisites at the domestic level: the criminalization of computer and computer-related offences and the creation of procedural powers to investigate and prosecute those committing such crimes. International cooperation mechanisms are a necessary response to cyber-crime, but not a sufficient one. A substantial portion of cyber-crime is transnational in nature, but some can happen at a purely domestic level. More importantly, it will usually be impossible to respond effectively to foreign requests for assistance unless adequate domestic powers covering criminal offences and investigative procedures are in place, and unless there are officials trained and equipped to administer and enforce them. The fight against cyber-crime has to start with the adoption of strong substantive and procedural legislation at the national

1   The author wishes to express her appreciation to Christopher D. Ram for this helpful comments and suggestions and to her colleagues Gareth Sansom, Catheryne Beaudette and Normand Wong for editing this paper. The views expressed in this paper may not necessarily represent the views of the Government of Canada or any department or agency thereof.

Ernesto U. Savona (ed.), Crime and Technology: New Frontiers for Regulations, Law Enforcement and Research, 39–54.

level. However, it is only by having all countries taking such steps that successful international cooperation can be achieved. A chain is only as strong as its weakest link: if even a few countries fail to adopt or enforce adequate measures, electronic "safe havens" are created which can be exploited by offenders.

After dealing with the challenges raised by cyber-crime, this paper will deal with both substantive offences and procedural powers that need to be adopted before a country can be relied upon to provide international cooperation. It will conclude with a brief look into the future of cyber-crime and the measures that will be needed to control it, while still maintaining the benefits of the technologies involved.

CHALLENGES AND POSSIBLE SOLUTIONS

States, as well as regional and international organizations, have been struggling to keep pace with the challenges created by rapidly evolving technologies. In general, these technologies make it more and more difficult to locate and gather the information and evidence required to carry out effective investigations and prosecutions in a single jurisdiction. At the same time, the technologies actually create new opportunities for investigators. They create and preserve information and other evidence that would not have existed before, but often require a high degree of training and sophistication on the part of investigators, and fully up-to-date legal powers, to take full advantage of the new opportunities and protect privacy and other human rights. To maximise the advantages and minimise the problems, a number of states have been putting their efforts together, developing different international or regional instruments to fight cyber-crime, and assisting one another in areas such as legislative development and the training of investigators.

The best known international legal instrument is the Council of Europe Convention on Cyber-crime (Council of Europe, 2001).[2] This treaty provides States Parties with legal tools to help in the investigation and prosecution of computer crime, including internet-based crime, and crime involving electronic evidence. The Convention calls for the criminalization of certain offences relating to computers, the adoption of procedural powers in order to investigate and prosecute cyber-crime, and the promotion of international cooperation through mutual assistance and extradition in a criminal realm that knows no borders. The Convention will help states fight crimes committed against the integrity, availability and confidentiality of computer systems and telecommunications networks as well as traditional offences committed using networks such as on-line fraud or the distribution of child pornography over the internet. It is open to countries outside Europe provided some basic requirements are met, and the four non-European countries which participated in the negotiation of the Convention – Canada, Japan, South Africa and the United States – are all in the process of ratifying it.

---

2   As of March 19, 2004, 32 countries had signed the Convention and 5 have ratified it. Texts, commentaries and the current status of the treaty can be found at: http://conventions.coe.int/Treaty/Commun/QueVoulezVous.asp?NT=185&CM=8&DF=8/4/04&CL=ENG (English versions).

The Commonwealth has also dealt with the issue of cyber-crime, primarily through model legislation developed to help its member states at the domestic level. The Model Law, entitled the Computer and Computer Related Crimes Act, was formally adopted by Commonwealth Law Ministers in 2002.[3] It has a common framework with the Council of Europe Convention on Cyber-crime, providing law enforcement with effective and modern tools to fight cyber-crime and other measures. Work has also been done at the international level by bodies concerned with specific crime-related issues such as the protection of children, and some international law requirements apply to specific cyber-crime issues. Notable examples include the involvement of UNICEF and UNESCO in promoting the protection of children from victimisation by child-pornographers and other forms of internet-related abuse (Amaldo, 2001). International legal instruments focused on specific issues tend to create general obligations which include but do not necessarily focus on cyber-crime issues. For example, article 34 of the UN Convention on the Rights of the Child (United Nations, 1989) requires States Parties to protect children from abuses such as child pornography and sexual exploitation whether these involve cyber-crime or not.

International responses to cyber-crime must also be seen in the broader context of international efforts to manage and regulate the technologies in general and for other specific purposes such as the establishment of standards and norms for electronic commerce and the use of digital evidence in non-criminal proceedings, which raise the further challenge of ensuring legal consistency and policy integration between criminal and non-criminal measures. In addition to the general management of the internet by the International Telecommunications Union (ITU), significant efforts have been made in this area by intergovernmental organizations such as the OECD and UN Commission on International Trade Law (UNCITRAL), in areas which include electronic evidence issues, taxation issues, privacy, security and trust issues and bridging the "digital divide" to ensure that developing countries are not excluded from new developments and opportunities (OECD, 2001) (UNCITRAL, 1996).

The solution to cyber-crime includes but is not limited to better international cooperation through the adoption of international or regional instruments to address the jurisdictional problems created by the borderless nature of computer networks. International cooperation is of no use if a country does not have in place the proper legal framework to first address the problem at the domestic level. Several of the major challenges posed by cyber-crime are at this level. Legislation setting out traditional offences needs to be adjusted to make it effective when the same offences are committed using information technologies, and new laws are often needed, especially for conduct in which the technologies and their users are themselves

---

3   See Commonweath (2002). For the text and reports on the 2001 and 2002 meetings at which the document was prepared see: http://www.thecommonwealth.org/shared_asp_files/uploadefiles/ {DA109CD2-5204-4FAB-AA77-86970A639B05}_Computer%20Crime.pdf. The author was a member of the Commonwealth group of experts which developed the Model Law. For other documents relating to the work of the Commonwealth in this area, see Commonwealth Secretariat, Legal and Constitutional Affairs Division at: http://www.thecommonwealth.org/Templates/Internal.asp? NodeID=38066.

targeted by offenders. Once adopted, keeping abreast of new technological developments is also essential, and this is a significant problem even for countries with a high
degree of socio-economic development and access to a high degree of technical
expertise. It will prove a much more serious problem for developing countries.
Finally, creating and maintaining the technical expertise needed to investigate and
prosecute offences at home and to respond quickly and effectively to requests
for cooperation in transnational cases is also a major demand, both on resources and
technical expertise.

It is essential that all states must take a multi-faceted approach. First, all states
need laws that will criminalize computer and computer-related crime by establishing
adequate definitions and offences in this respect. Second, they need to develop adequate procedural laws and training courses to allow for the timely and efficient investigation and prosecution of cyber-criminals. This implies the development of the
technical expertise needed to give effect to new procedural tools, in particular those
needed to obtain and preserve data and to ensure that it can be produced as evidence
in court. Finally, they need the commitment and capacity to improve international
cooperation in order to trace criminals on the internet and assist one another in the
conduct of transnational investigations and prosecutions.

SUBSTANTIVE LEGISLATION

a) The Principles

Without national legislation to deal with the use of computers as tools, storage devices
and targets, no international cooperation to fight cyber-crime is possible. However,
such legislation cannot be developed in a vacuum and needs to be harmonized from
one country to the other. Each country must apply its own legal framework, but
consistency between countries in their approaches to the framing of offences and
investigative powers and procedures greatly simplifies and expedites matters of mutual
legal assistance, extradition and other forms of cooperation. This is a major factor in
dealing with all forms of transnational crime, but will be particularly important in the
fast-moving investigations commonly required to deal effectively with cyber-crime
cases. As with international law, harmonization or consistency in domestic law is
important not just among the laws of different states, but also between criminal and
non-criminal laws and policies affecting information technologies.

Even more important is the requirement that each and every country must take
some action. Unlike most traditional forms of transnational crime, cyber-criminals
can commit offences in or through a country without ever actually going there themselves. This means that countries that do not have such legislation could become safe
havens and frustrate cyber-crime investigations and prosecutions at the international
level. Not only will this be damaging for the countries that are impacted by such
crimes, but those countries which are safe havens will certainly be challenged in their
domestic capacity to benefit from the widespread adoption of the internet. Even countries, in which the high technology sector is not a major player need to realize that
their economies, which are linked to the provision of essential services such as postal

or banking services, air traffic control and critical infrastructure protection, are certainly vulnerable to such crimes.

Developing adequate substantive offences requires focusing on the domestic legal framework at the outset, taking into account legal traditions. A "one size fits all" solution will not work. Rather, the solution lies in the harmonization of national legislation to ensure that while countries adopt measures that work effectively within their own national systems, they will still be able to provide cooperation to one another at the international level. A good approach is to develop a list of elements, which must be addressed in an offence or group of offences, and to use such a list as the outline for legislative drafting in accord with their national practice. This will generally support international cooperation, even if the resulting offences are not identical. Increasingly, the principle applied in instruments governing international cooperation, such as the United Nations conventions against corruption (United Nations, 2003) and transnational organized crime (United Nations, 2000), is that where dual criminality is required at all, it is the underlying conduct or basic elements of the offence which must correspond, and not the mere form or drafting of the offences in each country.

National legal perspectives may vary, but the impacts of illicit conduct are experienced similarly regardless of the jurisdiction. This reality is exaggerated in the context of cyber-crime where one criminal act may affect several jurisdictions simultaneously. Another important principle in drafting substantive offences is to ensure that these offences will not become obsolete as ever-newer technologies become available. While laws need to be continually reviewed to ensure their relevance to the changing environment, they should be drafted as much as possible in technology-neutral language that will stand the passage of time.

Substantive offences also need to be drafted bearing in mind that countries may not wish to criminalize conduct if it is done for legitimate purposes. For example, a person protecting his or her computer against cyber-attacks might be wilfully intercepting private communications – in other circumstances a criminal offence – in that context. Laws prohibiting the possession of devices designed primarily for the purpose of committing a computer crime may also apply to security devices possessed by computer professionals for security purposes. If the offence does not exclude conduct done with some legal justification or right or otherwise limit the scope of liability, offence provisions could be overbroad, encompassing legitimate activities and not adequately addressing the intended target of illicit or criminal activity. As an additional safeguard, because of the nature of computers and the possibility of persons interfering with or accessing data with lawful authority to do so, substantive offences should generally require a clear criminal intent for criminal liability to apply.

b) The Offences

Most countries today have understood the necessity of being able to prosecute crimes committed with the assistance of a computer, whether that crime was committed with a computer as a tool, a target or a storage device. Descriptions, classifications and typologies of illicit activities that should be criminalized or offences that have in fact been established in the domestic laws of many states can be found in a number of academic articles and international reports (Piragoff, 2003; Grabowski, 2001; Charney and Alexander, 1996; O'Neill, 2000; Sieber, 1986; United Nations, 2001).

In order to respond to the use of computers as tools in the commission of offences, states might not be required to enact legislation if the conduct prohibited by the specific offence is criminalized regardless of whether or not the offence is committed with the use of a computer. For example, countries wishing to address the growing problem of child pornography on the internet will want to make sure that their offences of distributing, making, printing, distributing and importing are equally applicable to any context. In Canada, although the latter offences did not require any modifications as they were equally applicable to a paper world and to data, the government believed that the creation of new offences of "transmitting", "accessing" and "making available" child pornography were required to bring the offences up to speed with new technologies, in particular the internet.

Another significant modification in relation to "communication offences" such as those related to child pornography and hate propaganda might be necessary in order to allow for a court to delete illegal material from a website situated within its jurisdiction. Such powers would be analogous to the existing authorities to seize, confiscate and destroy illicit tangible materials. While this does not prevent the same material from appearing in or from another jurisdiction if that other jurisdiction does not have similar legislation, it is a step toward reducing the availability of illegal material. Once again, it is worth repeating that it is only if all countries work together in harmonizing their legislation that any successful fight against cyber-crime will succeed.

Traditional offences such as theft, fraud and forgery might also require some amendments if they are only applicable to tangible documents. While the national concepts of such offences may differ significantly from one country to another, legislators should at least ensure that these offences will apply in the context of computers and computer networks.

Responses to the use of computers as storage devices in the commission of offences tends to involve the procedural powers to obtain and preserve electronic evidence (below), rather than criminal offence provisions, although adjustments to some offences such as those involving the concealment of evidence or obstruction of justice might have to be considered.

Addressing the problems of computers being the targets of crimes has required creativity by lawmakers since crimes against the integrity, availability and confidentiality of computer systems are complex, of a technical nature and somewhat different from traditional crimes in which a person suffers harm or damage. Both the Council of Europe Convention on Cyber-crime (articles 2–6) and the Commonwealth Model Law (articles 5–9) propose the creation of offences relating to illegal access, interfering with data, interfering with a computer, illegal interception of data and offences related to illegal devices.

PROCEDURAL LEGISLATION

a) The Principles

The second step in the fight against cyber-crime is to ensure that the appropriate procedural investigative powers are in place at the domestic level. This is essential both to ensure that domestic law enforcement officials have the powers they require to conduct domestic investigations and to ensure that they are able to take many of the same steps for purposes such as tracing criminal communications and to preserve, obtain and transmit electronic evidence when requested to do so by another country. One major problem with implementing these powers is related to the nature of computers in general and of the internet in particular. Before the advent of computers, most criminals were returning to the scene of the crime. Today, not only does the person committing a computer crime rarely return to that scene but, in most cases, that person will not even have been close to the place where the crime was committed. That person might be in another town, country or continent. Having in place adequate powers to allow investigators to follow the electronic tracks of a criminal is essential, and in no area of investigation is inter-operability between the national systems of different countries more important. Old legal tools will almost certainly have to be modified, entirely new ones may have to be created, and consensus among states as to what ought to be done and how, is, if not essential, then certainly a major advantage.

Not only do domestic authorities have to be able to trace the trail of a criminal, but they must do so in a timely fashion. The volatility of data and its intangible and transient nature lies at the heart of the problem. Law enforcement authorities need to have the tools necessary to find and safeguard the evidence of a crime, whether it is of a tangible or intangible nature. Electronic evidence can usually be destroyed at the touch of a keyboard. A related problem is the fact that communications can easily be – and frequently are – routed through many countries between source and destination, and such is the nature of the internet that fragments of the same communication may even have taken different routes. Communications must often be traced back through many countries, one after another, quickly enough so that electronic traffic data is not automatically erased before the tracing can be done.

b) The Powers

Every state's basic investigative powers need to be revisited by national authorities in order to make sure that they can be resorted to in the context of computer crime investigations and prosecutions. In countries where limits on the scope of a search for evidence are subject to strict limits as a procedural safeguard, these may have to be reconfigured or broadened to ensure computer systems can be searched effectively. For example, the traditional power of search and seizure might require a number of modifications to ensure that the place to be searched can include a computer system. When a network of computers in different cities is searched, at what "place" is the search conducted? What limits should be included in national legislation and how should those limits be dealt with at the international level? Should a domestic search power allow for a search in a territory outside the jurisdiction of the judge issuing the search warrant in circumstances in which the data is available through the computer system located in that jurisdiction? While sovereignty concerns might be raised by the way these questions are answered, some of the criticism addressed to current mutual legal assistance procedures might be alleviated.

Another problem from a law enforcement perspective arises from the complexity of computer systems, the volumes of data that they may contain, and the increasing prevalence of security measures to protect privacy and prevent unauthorized access to data. These factors have prompted a number of countries to adopt legislation to compel those in control of computer systems to use the systems themselves to search for and identify the target data, to produce it and to transfer it to those authorized to order its production, usually in a form that can be read and produced as evidence. Usually referred to as production orders, such powers have previously been enacted in a number of countries to allow for the obtaining of physical records, and are dealt with in both the Council of Europe Convention (article 18) and the Commonwealth Model Law (article 15). Countries already having such legislative powers in relation to physical documents might want to look at them again to make sure that the production orders can also be used to compel custodians to produce data and that the courts issuing such orders will do so under thresholds appropriate to the nature of the data or documents produced. For example, an order requiring a service provider to produce the information needed to identify customers or subscribers (subscriber information) or the traffic data needed to trace a communication might be issued at a lower standard than an order requiring the production of the actual content of the communications involved where these can be considered as private correspondence.

To balance the differing degrees of privacy expectation and the corresponding powers of search and seizure, cyber-crime experts and states have generally distinguished between data which are the content of actual communications, and "traffic data", which are the data used by the internet and other telecommunications systems to identify and locate the source and destination of communications so that messages and responses can be delivered, and which are needed by investigators to trace communications. A third category sometimes used is "subscriber data", which links the electronic addresses involved to the natural or legal persons actually using them. To use e-mail as an example, an e-mail message itself is seen as content, and subject to a high expectation of privacy. The message header or IP address used to deliver the message would be "traffic data", and the names, addresses and other personal information about the owners or users of the e-mail accounts (often held by service providers for billing purposes) would be "subscriber information". Both "traffic data" (article 1, subparagraph (d)) and "subscriber information" (article 18, paragraph 3) are defined in of the Council of Europe Convention.

The interception powers that were drafted for analog telephones may also need to be reviewed to ensure that they are applicable to the real-time tracing of content or traffic data on computer networks. Court authorizations need to be reconsidered to ensure that they can be obtained for both content and traffic data under appropriate standards reflecting the different expectation of privacy that persons have in relation to these two types of data. Countries which limit the issuance of court authorizations to intercept private communications to specific offences listed by statute or categories of serious offences or offences punishable by certain maximum sentences of imprisonment may need to reconsider this approach, as internet interceptions must often be done very quickly, before it may be apparent to investigators which offences are involved. By the time a specific offence can be identified, the opportunity to intercept or preserve data, especially traffic data, may have been lost.

As with any form of crime, an effective fight against cyber-crime requires that investigations be carried out in a timely manner, but the time-frames often become much more demanding where cyber-crime is involved. Many states have dealt with some of these problems by establishing more liberal requirements for the interception of traffic data than content data, as the former usually raises a lower expectation of privacy and is more likely to be lost if action is not taken quickly. Once the computers involved have been identified, higher standards and more time-consuming procedures can usually be undertaken to recover the content. It is important, therefore, that states ensure that traffic data can be quickly obtained through a court order issued under an appropriate standard for the investigation of all criminal offences and not only the most serious ones. As was mentioned earlier, it is more and more common that data contained in a computer may afford evidence of a number of types of crimes and not only evidence in relation to computer and computer related crimes.

Computer and telecommunications systems have become complex and contain vast quantities of data, making it difficult even for trained law-enforcement experts to successfully access the system, locate the target data and examine or copy it without causing harm to the system or other users. For this reason, in both the context of search and seizure and interception orders, countries might also want to consider how the assistance of third parties can be compelled. Assistance orders may be issued where a third party's assistance is reasonably required to give effect to these orders. The scope of such orders might need to be spelled out more clearly in order to deal adequately with challenges such as encryption or the provision of passwords, bearing in mind human rights, such as the right to be protected against self-incrimination.

Another important tool is the preservation order (Council of Europe Convention, article 16; Commonwealth Model Law, article 17), which deals with the fact that electronic data is particularly vulnerable to loss or modification. Typically, this procedural mechanism allows for the immediate safeguarding of stored data or documents in the control of the custodian, usually a service provider, in cases where law enforcement officers believe that such documents or data are relevant to a specific investigation or proceeding. Such a power usually operates as a "do-not-delete" order that will require the custodian of documents or data to save documents or data they currently have. The order is temporary, remaining in effect only as long as it takes law enforcement agencies to obtain judicial authority to seize the data or documents or a production order to deliver the data or documents. This is a stop-gap measure to ensure that information vital to a particular investigation, but that could have been deleted because of normal business practices, is preserved while the appropriate court order is obtained. This should not be confused with data retention requirements, under which legislation compels service providers to collect and retain a range of data concerning all subscribers for a set period, to ensure availability should its production later be required in a criminal case (Explanatory Report to the Council of Europe Convention, paragraph 151).

The expedited preservation and partial disclosure of traffic data, allows law enforcement authorities to request the disclosure of enough traffic data to be able to trace back all the service providers that were involved in the transmission of data particular to the investigation (Council of Europe Convention, article 17). This measure is one of the pre-requisites for adequate international cooperation since service providers located in several jurisdictions is the norm rather than the exception, and successful tracing of a communication usually requires the cooperation of every provider in the chain of transmission.

INTERNATIONAL COOPERATION

a) The Principles

Two pre-requisites are necessary for international cooperation to occur. First, as mentioned earlier, no international cooperation can occur without having in place, at the domestic level, the appropriate substantive offences and procedural powers. Second, the harmonization of domestic laws of different countries and the establishment of a legal framework on which cooperation can be requested and delivered is also essential. Harmonization of offences is needed for both mutual legal assistance and extradition where dual criminality is a requirement. An international legal framework (which may be multilateral, bilateral or even case-specific) provides a basis on which all of the countries involved play a role in determining whether the domestic legal requirements of the various countries concerned have been met. Extradition, for example, will be a matter for the courts of the state in which the offender is located, but extradition treaties, agreements or arrangements provide the basis for another state to request the extradition and to provide evidence or information needed to justify the extradition. Once these two pre-requisites are taken care of in domestic legislation, international cooperation is possible. Most often, international frameworks take the form of treaties or agreements, which cover a general range of subject matter, but increasingly, as with domestic legislation, these may have to be adjusted to take account of the unique nature of cyber-crime.

b) The Powers

The two main mechanisms that need to be looked at in order for a country to be able to contribute to the fight against cyber-crime at the international level are mutual legal assistance and extradition. Mutual legal assistance and extradition may be governed either by a treaty, an agreement or an arrangement. Treaties or agreements can be of general application, such as the United Nations Convention on Transnational Organized Crime, or subject-specific, such as the European Convention on Cyber-crime. The European Convention (article 23, *et seq.*) establishes a hybrid scheme in relation to international cooperation. While the Convention may serve as the basis to make requests if there is no existing treaty or to supplement provisions of existing treaties, existing treaties and arrangements take precedence. Such a scheme was believed to be important to states that negotiated the Convention since all states tailor their bilateral relations to take into account particular sensitivities or safeguards.

In order to fight cyber-crime, states have to find ways to provide for timely and efficient mutual legal assistance to the widest extent possible. Obtaining access to the legal investigative powers of another state is crucial to that goal. As mentioned earlier, the types of substantive offences for which mutual legal assistance should be granted are not only those related to the availability, integrity and confidentiality of a computer system, but any crime where computers can be used as storage devices for or repositories of evidence of any crime. The same principle applies for the procedural powers: international cooperation should be possible not only for the investigations or proceedings of computer and computer related offences, but also for the collection of evidence in electronic form of any crime (Council of Europe Convention, article 25, paragraph (1)).

A few words need to be said in relation to some of the possible modifications that need to be made for a state to be able to provide adequate mutual legal assistance in the context of cyber-crime. First, in relation to preservation orders for stored content or traffic data, which are probably even more important tools at the international than the national level, states should endeavour to remove their dual criminality requirement as it would be counter-productive to the timely investigations of cyber-crime. If such a requirement cannot be forborne in the context of cyber-crime, it should be saved only for the more intrusive investigative measures, such as searches or the interception of private communications. In addition, states should endeavour to better cooperate with each other in both the real-time collection of traffic data, as well as the interception of content data. Obviously, this requires a more profound rethinking of fundamental values as most states do not currently allow mutual legal assistance mechanisms in relation to these latter types of intercepts. Once again, it is the timeliness of such cooperation that will allow states to fight cyber-crime.

Mutual legal assistance mechanisms will not be sufficient, however, for states to successfully fight cyber-crime. While such mechanisms are useful to collect evidence and assist in identifying criminals, the prosecution and punishment of such persons may require the extradition of the fugitive to the state that has the jurisdiction, the means and the will to prosecute. Extradition schemes must therefore be reviewed to ensure that all computer and computer-related crimes are considered to be extraditable offences. In countries where a *de minimus* threshold applies to extradition cases (usually by excluding offences punishable by less than one year) substantive offence and sentencing provisions should ensure that the basic computer and computer-related crimes meet these requirements. For the States Parties to the Council of Europe Convention (article 24) such offences are deemed to be included in any existing treaties or other extradition arrangements. Consideration could also be given to ensuring that maximum punishments are four years or greater, in order to trigger application of the United Nations Convention against Transnational Organized Crime, where the other triggering requirements in articles 2 and 3 of that Convention are present.

CONCLUSION

Information and communications technologies have tremendous potential benefits. Most countries have come to recognize this and the acquisition and deployment of such technologies has become a key element of development strategies around the world. The extent to which they are present and available in a country has even become an important indicator of development (OECD, 2001a). Not all of the effects of the technologies are of a positive nature, however, and gaps in distribution and availability have prompted calls from the United Nations to bridge the "digital divide" (United Nations General Assembly, 2000: paragraphs 150–67). However, all countries have or will in the not so distant future feel their impact for better and for worse.

Given the projected growth of the internet and its number of users and the corresponding expansion in the use of new technologies and the internet to commit crimes, cyber-crime has proven a formidable challenge to all states, including even the most developed states, in which the companies, which develop and market the technologies, are located. It also poses a very serious challenge to the efforts of less developed countries as well in terms of accelerating the delivery of health care, education, electronic commerce and the like as part of their development strategies. For this reason, a number of countries, as well as international and regional organizations, have been addressing the challenges posed by the emergence of computers and the internet through the development of model legislation, technical assistance in drafting legislation, training of law enforcement officers, legislative drafters and policy makers and the establishment of links between governments and industry.

At the international level, the G8 has been active in this area mainly by adopting principles, recommendations and statements in relation to various aspects of high-tech crime (G-8, 1997, 1999, 2002, 2002a and 2002b), and in promoting a 24-hour, 7-day network of law enforcement cyber-crime units. Following the adoption by the Commonwealth of its 2002 Model Law, the Commonwealth Secretariat has held training seminars for drafters and policy makers to assist them in developing national legislation on this issue. The Organization of American States (OAS) is developing an integral OAS cyber-security strategy and will be holding regional legislative drafting workshops on cyber-crime. Asia-Pacific Economic Cooperation (APEC) is currently conducting a capacity-building project on cyber-crime for member economies in relation to legislative frameworks and investigative capabilities. APEC economies that are advanced in this respect will assist other member economies in developing legislation and forensic training. Finally, the United Nations has also adopted a number of resolutions on this issue over the last fifteen years (United Nations General Assembly, 2002a; United Nations General Assembly, 2002; United Nations General Assembly, 2001; United Nations, 1990: draft resolution 9 – computer-related crime; United Nations, 1994).

Computer-related crime is now a frequently-recurring agenda item for the United Nations Commission on Crime Prevention and Criminal Justice, taken up at the 10th, 11th, 12th and 13th sessions. In addition to Commission discussion of such crime as a transnational crime issue, specific reports were tabled at the 10th and 11th sessions (United Nations, 2001; United Nations, 2002). A workshop on crimes related to the computer network was held at the 10th U.N. Congress on the Prevention of Crime and the Treatment of Offenders (UNAFEI, 2001), and at the time of writing, planning was underway for a further workshop to be held at the 11th Congress in 2005. Further work in this area was called for by the 10th Crime Congress and the subsequent action-plan, but is contingent on the availability of resources and had generally not been carried out as of mid-2004 (United Nations General Assembly, 2000a: annex; United Nations General Assembly, 2002a: annex).

Within the Commission, some Member States have recently raised the idea of developing an international convention on cyber-crime, in addition to the need for technical assistance and other issues. The idea of developing an international convention on cyber-crime as a solution to the challenges faced by the international community as a whole in dealing with cyber-crime is interesting in many respects. While this discussion goes well beyond the scope of this paper, a few elements can be pointed out. On the one hand, the steady increase in global access to the internet and the resulting equally steady increases in cyber-crime can expect to increase pressure for a concerted international effort, including some form of international legal instrument as the basis or framework for such action. On the other hand, serious technical and legal problems will need to be addressed before such an instrument can be developed.

First, developing countries would have to be assisted in raising standards for technical security and investigative techniques from an operational perspective as such techniques may raise security concerns on the part of other governments, and in some cases concerns about economic interests and proprietary technologies among the companies which produce the technologies and the countries in which they are based. Second, human rights standards in areas such as privacy and the legal rights of persons facing criminal prosecution would have to be rationalised to support some of the closer forms of cooperation, such as cross-border or cooperative search and seizure operations, for example. An obvious related issue in this respect is how sovereignty concerns are addressed. Third, while the European Convention on Cyber-crime is open to non-European States, some countries may find that such an instrument does not suit their needs or specific circumstances. On the other hand, developing another international treaty will take time to negotiate in view of the different legal systems, stages of development and cultural backgrounds.

While the resolution of some of these issues is clearly not an immediate prospect, this need not delay work in all areas. Before work on a global legal instrument can begin, capacity-building efforts can be undertaken to ensure that when time is ripe for an instrument to be developed, all countries will have the expertise needed to implement it. The format used for the United Nations Convention against Transnational Organized Crime, in which core elements were included in a parent Convention, with additional specific crime problems dealt with in supplementary Protocols, also suggests a possible solution to some of the problems. It has also been suggested that a further Protocol to that Convention might be developed to deal with computer-related crime, but this would not be feasible, because a significant fraction of transnational computer-related crime does not necessarily involve any element of an organized criminal group and would thus be beyond the scope set by Articles 2 and 3, and applied to Protocols by Article 37, of the Convention. Many elements of the Convention could well be used in a future convention against computer-related crime, but some would require adjustments to take account of the circumstances which arise when major transnational crimes are committed by individuals or groups which are not connected in the ways envisaged by the existing Convention.

Another possible approach might be to develop a group or cluster of instruments, beginning in areas where consensus is possible, and supplementing this with further provisions in additional instruments later on. Much the same approach has been taken with respect to anti-terrorism treaties, with a series of specific treaties on subjects such as terrorist bombing and financing successfully concluded in the absence of any immediate consensus for a comprehensive treaty on terrorism.

Whether it takes the form of the Council of Europe Convention being ratified by a significant number of non-European States across the developing and developed world or an new international convention negotiated under the auspices of the United Nations, a clear international consensus is required on how all countries have to work together to fight cyber-crime. No government can afford ignoring these emerging crime trends or work in isolation in adopting domestic laws to deal with them. The new reality that we are facing today has changed forever the world we live in and we cannot afford to fight 21st century crime with tools put in place some centuries ago. This requires a new way of thinking and will challenge the rights and freedoms that more and more are taken for granted. The scepticism associated with achieving an international consensus on how to deal with cyber-crime will jeopardize one of the most important tools for sustainable development: the growth of electronic commerce.

In a nutshell, states need to react and start thinking more creatively. Not only does their national legislation need to be revisited regularly to ensure that they have the proper substantive offences and procedural tools in place to fight cyber-crime, but they also have to work together at the national and international levels with all stake-holders, including industry, in ensuring that the proper tools are in place to allow for more efficient and timely ways of providing international cooperation. As was mentioned by the Honourable Anne McLellan, former Minister of Justice of Canada, at the 10th United Nations Congress on the Prevention of Crime and the Treatment of Offenders:

> There are no simple solutions. Any effective solution will attack beliefs, which are fundamental to both countries and individuals. This is the key difficulty in developing practical and useful solutions to cyber-crime. The underlying reality is that any legislative measures we adopt, whether domestically or internationally, will have to involve a re-thinking of our basic notions of sovereignty, human rights and privacy. While it is imperative that we continue to protect all those rights, we must also recognize that our current notions were formed in a context that is much different from the world in which we live today.
>
> The landscape in which law enforcement now operates when investigating computer-related crime looks quite different from that of the past. We therefore have to adapt our laws and our deeply entrenched notions to accommodate this new reality. Without dispensing with our time-honoured conceptions of human rights and sovereignty, we must find a way to adapt these notions to a new environment so that they apply to the world in which we currently live.

In addition to creativity, our new challenges require courage. Courage to re-think our firmly held assumptions about how the world and our legal systems must operate, and courage to forge ahead with the bold steps necessary to confront the challenges facing us this new age. With creativity and courage, we can eventually overcome these challenges, make the internet safe and preserve our basic freedoms and values.[4]

This is what the fight against cyber-crime is all about.

REFERENCES

Amaldo, C.A. (ed.), *Child Abuse on the Internet: Ending the Silence*. Paris/New York/Oxford: UNESCO Publishing/Berghahn Books, 2001.

Charney, S. and K. Alexander, Legal Issues in Cyberspace: Hazards on the Information Highway. *Emory Law Journal*, 46, pp. 931–957, 1996.

Commonwealth, *Computer and Computer Related Crime Act* (*Model Law on Computer and Computer-Related Crime*) (LMM (02) 17), 2002.

Council of Europe, *Convention on Cyber-Crime*, 2001.

G-8, *Principles and Action Plan to Combat High-Tech Crime*, 1997.

G-8, *Principles on Transborder Access to Stored Computer Data*, 1999.

G-8, *Recommendations for Tracing Networked Communications Across National Borders in Terrorist and Criminal Investigations*, 2002.

G-8, *Principles on the Availability of Data Essential to Protecting Public Safety*, 2002a.

G-8, *G8 Statement on Data Protection Regimes and Data Preservation Checklists*, 2002b.

Grabowski, P., Computer Crime: A Criminological Overview. In: UN-CICP (Ed), *Forum on Crime and Society*, Vol. 1 Part 1, 2001.

OECD, *Policy Brief on Electronic Commerce*, 2001.

OECD, *Science, Technology and Industry Scoreboard 2001 – Towards a Knowledge-based Economy*, 2001a.

O'Neill, M.E., Old Crimes in New Bottles: Sanctioning Cybercrime. *George Mason Law Review*, 9, pp. 237–288, 2000.

Piragoff, D.A., Computer Crime and Other Crimes against Information Technology in Canada. *International Review of Penal Law*, 64, pp. 201–240, 1993.

Sieber, U., *The International Handbook of Computer Crime: Computer-related Economic Crime and the Infringements of Privacy*. New York: Wiley, 1986.

United Nations, *Convention on the Rights of the Child* (GA/RES/44/25). 20 November, 1989.

United Nations, *Report of the Eighth United Nations Congress on the Prevention of Crime and the Treatment of Offenders* (A/CONF.144/28/Rev.1). Havana, 1990.

United Nations, Manual on the Prevention and Control of Computer-Related Crime. *International Review of Criminal Policy*, 43–44, 1994.

United Nations, *Convention against Transnational Organized Crime* (Palermo Convention) (GA/RES/55/25). 15 November, 2000.

United Nations, *Report of the Secretary General to the Commission on Crime Prevention and Criminal Justice at its Tenth Session. Conclusions of the Study on Effective Measures to Prevent and Control High-technology and Computer-related Crime* (E/CN.15/2001/4). 30 March, 2001.

---

4   The text of the speech is available at http://canada.justice.gc.ca/en/news/sp/2000/doc_25311.html.

United Nations, *Report of the Secretary General to the Commission on Crime Prevention and Criminal Justice at its Eleventh Session. Effective Measures to Prevent and Control Computer-related Crime.* (E/CN.15/2002/8). 29 January, 2002.

United Nations, *Convention against Corruption* (GA/RES/58/4). 31 October, 2003.

United Nations Asia and Far East Institute (UNAFEI), *The Global Challenge of High-tech Crime* (proceedings of the 10th Crime Congress workshop). Tokyo: UNAFEI, 2001.

United Nations Commission on International Trade Law (UNCITRAL), *Model Law on Electronic Commerce*, 1996. [available at: http://www.uncitral.org/english/texts/electcom/ml-ecomm.htm].

United Nations General Assembly, *We the Peoples: the Role of the United Nations in the Twenty-first Century* (Millennium Declaration) (A/54/2000). 27 March, 2000.

United Nations General Assembly, *Vienna Declaration on Crime and Justice: Meeting the Challenges of the Twenty-first Century* (GA/RES/55/59). 4 December, 2000a.

United Nations General Assembly, *Combating the Criminal Misuse of Information Technologies* (A/RES/55/63). 22 January, 2001.

United Nations General Assembly, *Combating the Criminal Misuse of Information Technologies* (A/RES/56/121). 23 January, 2001.

United Nations General Assembly, *Plans of Action for the Implementation of the Vienna Declaration on Crime and Justice: Meeting the Challenges of the Twenty-first Century* (A/RES/56/261), Part XI (Action against high-technology and computer-related crime). 15 April, 2002a.

CHAPTER 5

NEW CHALLENGES FOR LAW ENFORCEMENT

Gloria Laycock

INTRODUCTION

This paper is based upon a presentation given at an international conference in Courmayeur, Italy, in November 2003. The conference was entitled 'Crime and Technology: New Frontiers for Regulation, Law Enforcement and Research'. It provided an opportunity to review the effects of technology on all aspects of crime – both the extent to which technological developments contribute to crime and also to the ways in which technology can help to prevent or detect it. The presentation was intended for a general audience and this paper is not, therefore, a research paper, but it does raise some issues of policy relevance to an international journal. It concentrates specifically on new challenges for law enforcement and how these might be dealt with. The basic thesis of the paper is that there are new and emerging crimes that require a more systematic and better co-ordinated approach than has been evident hitherto. Of course crime necessarily changes with time and circumstance; as Ken Pease (personal communication) says, horse thieves have been replaced in large part by car thieves, and there are many more of them. But with the rate of change of technological innovation, and the globalisation of industry, the opportunities for crime are rising at an unprecedented rate and there is, therefore, an urgency to the need for a more appropriate response to crime and disorder.

The argument will be that we need to take a more scientific approach in responding to the rising crime rates, and in the process encourage the technological developments to which they give rise. Although it is clear that we must retain the Criminal Justice System (CJS) as a significant element in crime policy it is also clear that it is not coping well with these new challenges. This paper argues that we should respond by more consciously embracing scientific method in attempting to control crime. This is about the use of data, logic, evidence and rationality. It is about testing hypotheses and establishing knowledge. It has been seen by some social scientists as overly positivist and inclined to draw firm conclusions on the basis of quantitative data, which ignores the qualitative context of social phenomena. But science has moved a

This chapter was previously published in *European Journal on Criminal Policy and Research* **10**: 39–53, 2004.

Ernesto U. Savona (ed.), Crime and Technology: New Frontiers for Regulations, Law Enforcement and Research, 55–68.
© 2004 *Springer. Printed in The Netherlands.*

long way from this position, if it were ever true. Science may be about discipline and measurement but it is also about discovery and creativity. It is essentially about probability and understanding what can and cannot be concluded on the basis of observation and experimentation. There is relatively little real experimentation in the crime control field. (See Sherman (2003) for a review, which concentrates specifically on the paucity of randomised controlled trials research in the social sciences. The lack of experimentation, however, applies more widely.)

Experimentation is only one aspect of science that could prove useful. Science can help us to understand crime and its causes by systematically observing, describing and categorising the behaviours which society chooses to proscribe. Insights so derived can open up new possibilities for responding to crime and disorder, that take account of the realities of crime rather than the sometimes dogmatic assumptions of politicians. Science can also, through the technologies that are developed from it, help us to make crimes more difficult to commit by preventing them from happening in the first place, and it can help us to catch offenders more quickly and bring them to justice more reliably. More generally, thinking scientifically should increase our knowledge and facilitate an evidence-based approach to crime control.

The paper is divided into five sections. In the second section, on the new challenges, there is a brief discussion of the crime context and some of the challenges now faced in dealing with offending. The third section, on the case for prevention looks at elements of what is already known about the nature of crime and the implications for crime control on the basis of scientific research that has already been completed. It makes the case for prevention. 'Science and detection', the fourth section, looks briefly at how science and technology might contribute to improving detection rates and finally, the fifth section, on implications for crime control policy and policing, considers the implications of what has been discussed for crime control policy and policing.

THE NEW CHALLENGES

Although toward the end of the 20th century, crime rates appeared to be decreasing in many advanced western democracies, overall the rates remain unacceptably high (Van Kesteren et al. 2000). Furthermore, insofar as crime decreased in the 1990s there is no clear explanation about how this happened (see, for example, Blumstein and Wallman 2000). It is therefore difficult to argue that governments or law enforcement agencies were in control of the situation (although this, of course, has not stopped many of them from claiming credit for the apparent reductions).

There are a number of reasons for the crime rates that we perceive. First, although absolute poverty reduced throughout the 20th century, some commentators feel that there is a growing gap between rich and poor, which has been said to fuel crime. Secondly, in the immediate past, in the UK at least, there has been an increase in truancy rates amongst young people and a perceived disaffection with the education system, which in turn leads to difficulties in finding quality employment and no 'buy in' to the wider social system. Parenting skills come under scrutiny from time to time and are seen as contributing to the increased offending of young people exacerbated by a high rate of single parent households. Drugs also play a part in the crime rates that we observe – with drug taking constituting an offence in its own right as well as driving shop theft, burglary and car crime as addicts try to raise money to fund their addictions. Finally, we have witnessed massive movements of populations, following jobs, with the breakdown of traditional communities and the familiarity and support that they offer. We now have enlarged and more complex social systems. Altogether a plethora of socially rooted problems many of which are themselves described as 'wicked issues' (Clarke and Stewart 1997) and which have a tendency to leave practitioners and citizens feeling that they are at the whim of major social forces over which they have little control.

Significantly, failure to deal with these intractable issues focuses crime control on the offender. The emphasis is on catching, treating, punishing, or deterring those who offend or those at risk of offending and this, in turn leads to the investment, which we see across Europe, in the CJS.

Over the last few decades the advocates of situational crime prevention (Clarke 1983) have challenged this emphasis on the CJS as the primary means of government sponsored crime control. Whilst acknowledging the importance of the wider social context, situational crime prevention places emphasis on the immediate situation as itself a *cause* of crime. From this perspective it is clear that the rapid development of new products and services, while welcome in themselves as a concomitant of successful capitalist economies, also provide new opportunities for crime. These new products may be the targets of theft but they may also facilitate offending by making offences easier to commit or making detection more difficult. The increased services can also offer new opportunities for offending if they are not designed with crime prevention in mind.

We see, then, high crime rates and relatively low detection rates. We also find increased difficulty in tackling what is commonly called organized crime, where there are more sophisticated but loosely connected networks of offenders taking advantage of systems such as the internet to commit their offences with relative impunity. Many of these challenges have emerged within the last few decades with the huge increase in and availability of technological products.

The next section looks at some of the evidence in support of a greater emphasis on preventing crimes from happening in the first place rather than reacting to offences already committed. It draws on research that helps us to understand the nature of crime and thus assists in informing new ways of dealing with it.

THE CASE FOR PREVENTION

Although we have known for at least a century that offending is common, particularly amongst young males, Gabor (1994) has shown that it is far *more* common than is normally thought, and that it is by no means restricted to young males. Gabor quotes a study as early as 1947 (Wallerstein and Wyle 1947), which showed that 90% of men and 80% of women in New York City committed larceny or theft at some point. Since that time there have been numerous studies showing the high rate of offending of the general public. An international self report study reported by Junger-Tas et al. (1994) showed, for example, that 66% of 14–21-year-olds in England and Wales would admit to ever having committed an offence with the comparable figures of 85% in the Netherlands, 81% in Portugal and Spain and 90% in Switzerland.

The picture from official crime data may be less depressing but it is still significant. UK research has shown, for example, that about 33% of the adult male population will have a criminal conviction by the age of 46. Of these half are convicted only once and just over half have a criminal career of less than a year. Nearly half will have been convicted of theft or handling stolen goods (Barclay and Tavares 1999). So although we are not talking about serious crime and it does not last for long in each individual case, there is a great deal of it.

These well-known research results are quoted here to make the point that young people do not offend on this scale because they are wicked but because of the situations within which they find themselves. We know from decades of psychological research of the power of the situation in determining behaviour. What we do is the product of an interaction between the kinds of people we are and the situation within which we find ourselves. And it is easier to change situations than it is to change dispositions, so research on situational crime prevention has concentrated on investigating how this can be done. Such an approach is a significant switch from the more usual policy of crime control with its heavy reliance on the CJS.

One element of the situation is the increasing prevalence of goods that are attractive to the potential thief. Such goods fit Clarke's (1999) acronym CRAVED. They are concealable, removable, available, valuable, enjoyable and disposable. Goods fitting this acronym will be more likely to be stolen. As Figure 1 shows, the effect of this can be seen when data from the British Crime survey are examined. The figure takes a selection of items stolen in the course of household burglaries over successive sweeps of the survey from 1984 to 2000. It illustrates the consistent vulnerability of

FIGURE 1. Trends in items stolen.

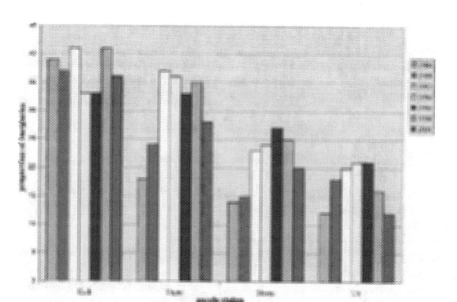

cash, which is perhaps the best fit for Clarke's acronym. It also demonstrates the change in vulnerability of television sets (and to a lesser extent videos and stereos) to burglary. This is perhaps because the market for stolen TVs is now less than it once was. The extent to which goods are vulnerable changes over time and this is something that can be manipulated (Felson 2002).

The change in vulnerability has been described by Pease (1997) as reflecting the crime cycle. We first find innovation in the design of goods or services with the crime consequences neglected. This leads to a crime harvest on the part of offenders who take advantage of the vulnerability of the goods or services. Security is then retrofitted or the service delivery is redesigned, and the relevant crime reduces.

Cornish and Clarke (2003) have described five major ways of addressing the vulnerability of goods and services – increase the effort required by the offender to commit the offence, increase the risk to the offender, reduce the rewards, reduce provocations or remove the excuses. Within each category are a further five techniques as shown in Table 1. These build on earlier work by Clarke, Homel and Wortley in developing this classification.

There are now numerous examples of the success of these techniques in reducing crime; some of which are described in the Crime Prevention Studies series of books edited by Clarke. For example:

- If new homes are 'secured by design', then burglary rates are 30% lower than homes that are otherwise matched but do not meet the secured by design standard (Armitage 2000).
- Alcohol-related violence was reduced to around a quarter of its previous level by changes to transport, food availability, entertainment choices and control of binge drinking (Homel et al. 1997).

TABLE 1. Twenty-five opportunity reducing techniques of situational crime prevention.

Increasing perceived effort	Increasing perceived risk	Reducing anticipated rewards	Reduce provocations	Removing excuses
1. Target hardening	6. Extend guardianship	11. Conceal targets	16. Reduce frustrations and stress	21. Set rules
2. Access control	7. Assist natural surveillance	12. Remove targets	17. Avoid disputes	22. Post instructions
3. Screen exits	8. Reduce anonymity	13. Identify property	18. Reduce emotional arousal	23. Alert conscience
4. Deflect offenders	9. Utilise place managers	14. Disrupt markets	19. Neutralise peer pressure	24. Assist compliance
5. Control tools/ weapons	10. Strengthen formal surveillance	15. Deny benefits	20. Discourage imitation	25. Control drugs and alcohol

Adapted from Cornish and Clarke (2004).

- Regularly cleaning Graffiti from the trains in the New York Subway eventually stopped the problem (Sloan-Howitt and Kelling 1992).
- Anti-robbery screens reduced robbery in sub-post offices (Ekblom 1987).
- In 1995 mobile phone cloning in the USA was costing $800 million. A whole raft of electronic counter measures taken by the industry all but eliminated such losses by the end of the 1990s (Clarke et al. 2001).

Many of these successful case studies adopted a problem solving approach to the offences in question. That is, they collect detailed data on the crime or disorder issue in question, hypothesise about the situational factors that contribute to the observed events and develop a response based on the theory that offenders make simple but basically rational choices in deciding whether, where and when to offend. The response might typically be related to one or more of the techniques outlined in Table 1.

In an ideal world the proponents of situational crime prevention would be able to experiment in a more systematic manner. In practice, they have had to be rather opportunistic themselves in seeking out examples of the successful application of these techniques. The introduction of laws requiring that riders of motor bikes wear helmets had the fortuitous effect of reducing the theft of motor bikes in the UK (Mayhew et al. 1989). Because similar legislation had been enacted in Germany, and because there were better data available there, it was possible for the researchers to specifically test for displacement. To quote the conclusion in their paper: 'As was predicted, the introduction of penalties for riding a motorcycle without protective headgear had the same unintended result in the Federal Republic of Germany as in England and the Netherlands of producing a substantial drop in the theft of motorcycles. More importantly, there was little evidence of displacement ...' (Mayhew et al. 1989: 6, italics added). That these 'experiments' were not contrived by the 'experimenter' does not detract from the predictions that were made and certainly does not negate the conclusion that situational crime prevention works. Taking advantage of such naturally occurring experiments clearly does not absolve the researcher from ensuring that the conclusions drawn are based on sound scientific principles, which control for chance and bias in interpretation. It makes the application of those principles more challenging, but not impossible.

Insofar as problem solving along these lines relates to policing specifically, it has been called problem-oriented policing (POP) (Goldstein 1990) although it can be applied by any agency, organisation or partnership wishing to tackle crime and disorder, in which case it is seen as an integral part of situational crime prevention. It could also be described more broadly as scientific method, and as such is a standard approach scientists take to a proportion of their work – What exactly is the nature of the problem? How could it be solved? How would it be hypothesised that the solution might work? Can the proposed solution then be applied and tested? And so on.

However characterised, the approach has proved difficult to embed into routine police practice (Scott 2000; Knutsson 2003). Goldstein (2003) suggests five reasons for this as set out below:

1. The absence of a long-term commitment on the part of police leaders to strengthening policing and the police as an institution.

2. The lack of skills within a police agency that is required to analyse problems and to evaluate strategies for dealing with those problems.
3. The lack of a clear academic connection.
4. The absence of informed outside pressures.
5. The lack of financial support.

These reasons apply most readily to the US context with which he is most familiar. In Europe there are some significantly different issues, and there is probably little uniformity across the continent. For example, the police agencies in Northern Europe, particularly in the UK and the Scandinavian countries are generally familiar with POP and sympathetic to the approach. In the UK there is, for example, an annual award (the Tilley Award) for the best police problem-solving project. In Southern Europe the policing style is more militaristic and less inclined toward problem solving. These are major cultural differences in approach and pose huge challenges to the development of European policing. This is particularly significant if there are aspirations to the development of a pan-European style of policing as the Community integrates and enlarges.

Notwithstanding the implementation difficulties, problem-solving and situational crime prevention have been demonstrated to work effectively. Specifically, changing situations as a means of crime control also appears to work without significant displacement of crime from one area, type, time or method (Barr and Pease 1990). There are a number of ethical issues which might benefit from wider public exposure but they do not, in themselves deliver a *coup de grace* to the approach (see for example, Von Hirsch et al. (2000) for a discussion of some key areas).

It remains, however, a marginal approach to crime control in the official government policies of many jurisdictions, where the crime reduction emphasis stays focussed on the offender – capture, trial and imprisonment or some other suitable disposal. One of the reasons that the CJS approach is less successful than it might be in crime control terms is because the first step is poorly executed – not enough offenders are caught. This again is an area in which a more scientific approach may prove beneficial.

SCIENCE AND DETECTION

Thanks to developments in science, there are now a number of techniques available to the police and other law enforcement agencies to assist in crime detection. It is possible, for example, to spray intruders who may have broken into a building with 'smart water', which is subsequently detectable under ultra-violet light. This allegedly helps in identifying offenders and linking them to crime scenes (see the manufacturer's website at http://www.smartwater.com/products/indexsol.html). Sensors, alarms and closed circuit television (CCTV) systems are also becoming increasingly sophisticated and can make use of computer technology to search for particular patterns of behaviour and raise the alarm.

In the UK, CCTV has been widely adopted on the basis of firm political conviction that it works. This conviction has only partially been borne out by research results

(Welsh and Farrington 2002), which show that sometimes crime goes down and sometimes it does not; it depends on the context and the method of implementation. This is a good example of the need for a multi-disciplinary approach to public policy development. The CCTV technology has been implemented in a wide range of different settings – in car parks, city centres, on housing estates and on public transport systems. Whether the technology works in delivering a crime reduction or not needs to be determined by a proper analysis of the various situations in which it has been introduced. This might call for the skills of a social scientist, working alongside the technologists or operational researchers responsible for installing and developing the systems.

One of the most long-standing scientific aids to detection is fingerprint technology, which was used throughout most of the 20th century. Copies of offenders' fingerprints are taken routinely in most advanced jurisdictions and records are kept. Until relatively recently these prints were examined by eye – a labour intensive and slow process. But with advanced computer technology it is now possible to examine prints electronically, which means that far more samples can be searched as a matter of routine. Again, it is not clear whether this technology is making a real difference to the detection of crime. In principle it should, but in practice there is not sufficient research evidence available to prove the point. So these technological developments which might support detection, need to be properly assessed in terms of their effectiveness.

A more recent development, which compares with fingerprint technology, is DNA. The remainder of this section concentrates on a discussion of this approach, as it raises some important issues for the development of the field, and in the context of this paper, produces challenges to policy and practice, which have yet to be fully addressed.

In the UK, DNA samples can be taken from anyone arrested for an offence. These samples can then be retained on the national DNA database, which was established in 1995, and is managed by the Forensic Science Service. Samples from crime scenes are searched against those on the database in order to link the sample (and thus the offender) with other offences, or to place an offender at a particular crime scene. The national DNA database currently holds over two million records. It is now reported on the Forensic Science Service website that in a typical month the database links suspects to 15 murders, 31 rapes and 770 car crimes. In 2002, 21,000 crimes were detected using DNA evidence – a 132% increase on 2000. The Home Office is funding an expansion of the database with an investment of £182 million from April 2000 to 2004 (see Forensic Science Service 2003).

This is seen by law enforcement agencies as a major advance in the scientific support of crime detection but it is not without its critics. Some argue that the ability to take DNA samples from all arrested offenders and retain the samples is a serious infringement of human rights. Liberty, the major UK human rights organisation, for example, has been highly critical of the developments. One of the first challenges then is to secure the integrity of these large and developing databases and to ensure that the information they contain is not misused by those with access to them. A second issue, which might threaten the integrity of the approach, comes under the general category of offender learning. There is some evidence, much of it anecdotal at this stage, that offenders, alert to the potential of DNA as a useful source of evidence, contaminate crime scenes with the DNA of other people. They also make a greater attempt to remove DNA traces by, for example, setting fire to stolen vehicles or requiring rape victims to wash following an offence. These are clearly adverse consequences but on the positive side, there is again anecdotal evidence that they may confess to crimes sooner or more readily if faced with the forensic evidence provided by DNA. Also on the positive side is the increasing evidence that convicted offenders have been able to successfully challenge their convictions on the basis of DNA evidence. These offences are often at the serious end of the continuum. In the USA, for example, a study commissioned by the former US Attorney General and published in 1996 found 28 convicted felons who had been exonerated following presentation of DNA evidence (Connors et al. 1996).

Of course these major advances in science and technology are of limited use if they are not implemented properly, and a significant element of implementation is training. A UK study by Tilley and Ford (1996) showed how relatively little understanding of forensic science there was on the part of police officers across the ranks. Figure 2, taken from their report illustrates this. A number of officers of various ranks and with different levels of experience of forensics were given a set of questions to test their knowledge and understanding. The figure shows the number who gave correct, valid or incorrect answers to the questions. Not surprisingly the senior scenes of crime officers and senior investigating officers did best, but even they were not always right.

Training needs go more widely than the police however. The judiciary and other members of the criminal justice system, including members of juries in some cases, have a poorly developed understanding of probability, odds ratios and population characteristics, which are arguably necessary to the appropriate use of some of the scientific approaches now available.

FIGURE 2. Mean awareness scores by rank.

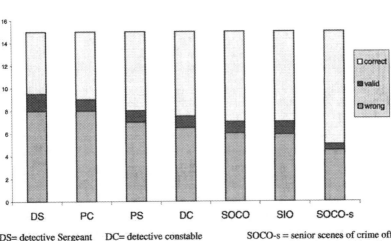

DS= detective Sergeant   DC= detective constable   SOCO-s = senior scenes of crime officer
PC= police constable   SOCO= scenes of crime officer
PS= police sergeant   SIO= senior investigating officer   (from Tilley and Ford, 1997, p.14)

There are then, a number of issues associated with the development of scientific techniques in the detection field, which need to be addressed. They imply a need for a greater integration between social and other sciences. It is the social sciences that can contribute to ethical debates on the use of science and technology, and alert us to possible disadvantages to their extended use. Techniques from the social sciences can also improve training programmes and management practices.

IMPLICATIONS FOR CRIME POLICY AND POLICING

Some of the implications of better integrating a scientific approach into crime control policy are profound. It seems clear that governments do not do enough to develop a context within which crime is made more difficult, a context within which the opportunities for crime are brought under control. We have seen an unprecedented expansion in the development of new technologies, many of which have contributed to the growth in crime. When those developing new goods or services bear the costs of crime, then there is an inbuilt incentive to consider the crime consequences, and in those situations we do see the fairly rapid development of counter-measures (an example is provided by Clarke et al. (2001) in relation to mobile phone cloning). But where the costs of crime are more diffuse, perhaps spread across a significant part of the general population and at relatively little unit cost, then there is little incentive for the development of goods with inbuilt security.

Perhaps the best example of this from the UK is car theft, where the increased security on motor vehicles was given a boost with the publication of the UK Car Theft Index (Houghton 1992). Laycock and Tilley (1995) described the way in which the manufacturers were persuaded to improve car security more fully. It required the UK government to take a more proactive approach and to develop a 'lever' over the manufacturers, which encouraged them to take car security much more seriously. The consequent reductions in the theft of vehicles, of the order of 30% over 10 years, have been attributed in large part to improvements in vehicle security (Laycock 2004).

Developing incentives for commerce and industry to 'think thief' (Ekblom 1997) when designing new products is one of the challenges for central governments. In our present stage of development, with increasing globalisation, nation states find it difficult to pressure multinational companies, even where they have the will to do so, to behave in what might be considered socially responsible ways during product development. In the car theft example, noted above, the media was used to publicise those manufacturers that were particularly vulnerable to criticism for the lack of security in their vehicles. A more direct measure might have been legislation but in the early 1990s it would have been necessary to engage other countries across the EU in order to achieve the necessary legislative change. At that time such proposals did not enjoy wide support. Times have changed and there are now EU directives on the security requirements for vehicles. But legislation is a slow process for achieving compliance and it would clearly be preferable if industries were alert to the crime consequences of poor design and planned accordingly. Car crime is, of course, only one example of offending that can be addressed by improved design and generally there is no systematic approach to this issue by governments at any level.

TABLE 2. Government responsibilities and crime control.

It is the responsibility of government to create a context within which we can *all* take responsibility for crime reduction, as individuals, as members of communities as directors of commerce and industry. This means, inter alia:

- Providing an efficient and effective criminal justice system
- Encouraging the reporting of crime and the attendance in court of victims and witnesses
- Encouraging us *all* to take responsibility
- Ensuring that all those with the *competency* to contribute to crime prevention do so

Adapted from Laycock (in press).

Table 2 (taken from 2004) is a first step in setting out some of the possible responsibilities of national governments for crime control. The suggestions in the table are based on the assumption that the primary responsibility for criminal behaviour lies at the individual level, but that those individuals cannot act on that responsibility if the social context does not support them. So, for example, while I maybe quite prepared to lock the door when leaving my car I have to rely on the manufacturers to provide a suitably secure lock. If they are disinclined to do this, for whatever reason (and it could be as simple as lack of forethought), then I must rely on the national government to pressurise them and to ensure that they do take appropriate action in the design of their goods.

The table refers specifically to nation states but could apply equally well to a larger union of nations such as the European Union or United Nations. Indeed, in the context of globalisation and multi-national companies, it is difficult to see how such companies might be persuaded to consider the crime consequences of some of their products if the consequences are not to be brought to their attention by such 'super-states', acting in the interest of consumers.

This is, however, easily said but difficult to see happening given the scale of vested interests involved. The idea that crime is the sole responsibility of criminals and that attention to the situation is somehow absolving the offenders of responsibility for their actions is pervasive. It is also in the interests of those manufacturers and industrialists who might prefer to continue to make and market their goods with little regard to the crime consequences. There is a sense in which it is comfortable to have responsibilities fall in this way. But it is becoming increasingly untenable to maintain this line when innovations such as the internet offer a profusion of crime control opportunities and little option for containment other than the design, or redesign, of the system itself (Newman and Clarke 2003).

The police have a role to play in this scenario. By taking a problem-solving, or more scientific approach to their work, they will be able to point to emerging crime opportunities more quickly and communicate their observations to a level at which action can be initiated. This is clearly idealistic but at present it is not even aspirational for most police agencies, which do not approach the policing task in this way. There is then, a major training task that encompasses the police and the analysts who support them if this new approach is to take root.

If there were a more systematic approach to opportunity management as set out here then the policing task should ultimately be easier – there should be less crime. That is not to say that crime control on these lines is a one-off effort. Offenders learn; they can soon overcome many security devices and new products are constantly being developed, so opportunistic offending is not going to stop. Furthermore there will still be a number of determined offenders who need to be caught. Here again there is a significant training need for the police in using the new technologies to best effect. The rate at which new products in support of police detection are coming onto the market place is such that there is an almost constant need for training and support. There are clear training gaps that need to be filled but which, in the longer-term, might offer a more effective, efficient and socially acceptable style of policing.

REFERENCES

Armitage, R., *An Evaluation of Secured by Design Housing in West Yorkshire,* Home Office Briefing Note 7/00. London: Home Office, 2000.

Barclay, G.C. and C. Tavares, *Information on the Criminal Justice System in England and Wales*, Digest 4. London: Home Office, 1999.

Barr, R. and K. Pease, Crime placement, displacement, and deflection. In: M. Tonry and N. Morris (Eds), *Crime and Justice: A Review of Research*, Vol. 12. Chicago: The University of Chicago Press, 1990.

Blumstein, A. and J. Wallman (Eds), *The Crime Drop in America*. Cambridge and New York: Cambridge University Press, 2000.

Clarke, R.V., Situational crime prevention: Its theoretical basis and practical scope. In: M. Tonry and N. Morris (Eds), *Crime and Justice: A Review of Research*, Vol. 4. Chicago: The University of Chicago Press, 1983.

Clarke, R.V., *Hot Products: Understanding, Anticipating and Reducing Demand for Stolen Goods*, Police Research Series, Paper 112. London: Home Office Research Development and Statistics Directorate, 1999.

Clarke, R.V., R. Kemper and L. Wyckoff, Controlling cell phone fraud in the US: Lessons for the UK 'Foresight' prevention initiative. *Security Journal*, 14(1), pp. 7–22, 2001.

Clarke, M. and J. Stewart, *Handling the Wicked Issues – a Challenge for Government*. Birmingham: University of Birmingham, 1997.

Connors, E., T. Lundregen, N. Miller and T. McEwan, *Convicted by Juries, Exhonerated by Science: Case Studies in the Use of DNA Evidence to Establish Innocence after Trial.* Washington, DC: US Department of Justice, Office of Justice Programs, 1996.

Cornish, D.B. and R.V. Clarke, Opportunities, precipitators and criminal decisions: A reply to Wortley's critique of situational crime prevention. In: M.J. Smith and D.B. Cornish (Eds), *Theory for Practice in Situational Crime Prevention*, Crime Prevention Studies, Vol. 16. Cullompton: Willan Publishing, 2003.

Ekblom, P., *Preventing Robberies at Sub-Post Offices*, Crime Prevention Unit Paper 9. London: Home Office, 1987.

Ekblom, P., Gearing up against crime: A dynamic framework to help designers keep up with the adaptive criminal in a changing world. *International Journal of Risk, Security and Crime Prevention*, 2, pp. 249–265, 1997.

Felson, M., *Crime and Everyday Life*. Thousand Oaks: Sage Publications, 2002.

Forensic Science Service, *The National DNA Database Annual Report 2002–03*. Forensic Science Service Communications Department, 2003.

Gabor, T., *Everybody Does It: Crime by the Public*. Toronto: University of Toronto Press, 1994.

Goldstein, H., *Problem-Oriented Policing*. New York: McGraw Hill, 1990.

Goldstein, H., On further developing problem-oriented policing: The most critical need, the major impediments, and a proposal. In: J. Knutsson (Ed.), *Problem-Oriented Policing From Innovation to Mainstream*, Crime Prevention Studies, Vol. 15. Cullompton: Willan Publishing, 2003.

Homel, R., M. Hauritz, R. Wortley, G. McIlwain and R. Carvolth, Preventing alcohol related crime through community action: The surfers paradise safety action project. In R. Homel (Ed.), *Policing for Prevention: Reducing Crime, Public Intoxication and Injury*, Crime Prevention Studies, Vol. 7. New York: Criminal Justice Press, 1997.

Houghton, G., *Car Theft in England and Wales: The Home Office Car Theft Index*, Police Research Group Crime Prevention Series, Paper 33. London: Home Office, 1992.

Junger-Tas, J., G.-J. Terlouw and M.W. Klein (Eds), *Delinquent Behaviour Among Young People in the Western World: First Results of the International Self-Report Delinquency Study*. Dordrecht: Kluwer Academic Publishers, 1994.

Knutsson, J. (Ed.), *Problem-Oriented Policing From Innovation to Mainstream*, Crime Prevention Studies, Vol. 15. Cullompton: Willan Publishing, 2003.

Laycock, G., The UK car theft index: An example of government leverage. In: M.G. Maxfield and R.V. Clarke (Eds), *Understanding and Preventing Car Theft*, Crime Prevention Studies, Vol. 17. Cullompton: Willan Publishing, 2004.

Laycock, G. and N. Tilley, Implementing crime prevention programs. In: M. Tonry and D. Farrington (Eds), *Building a Safer Society: Strategic Approaches to Crime Prevention – Crime and Justice: A Review of Research*, Vol. 19. Chicago: The University of Chicago Press, 1995.

Mayhew, P., R.V. Clarke and D. Elliott, Motorcycle Theft, Helmet Legislation and Displacement. *The Howard Journal of Criminal Justice*, 28(1), pp. 1–8, 1989.

Newman, G.R. and R.V. Clarke, *Superhighway Robbery: Preventing e-Commerce Crime*. Cullompton: Willan Publishing, 2003.

Pease, K., Predicting the future: The roles of routine activity and rational choice theory. In: G. Newman, R.V. Clarke and S. Shoham (Eds), *Rational Choice and Situational Crime Prevention*. Aldershot: Dartmouth, 1997.

Scott, M.S., *Problem-Oriented Policing: Reflections on the First 20 Years*. Washington, DC: Office of Community-Oriented Policing Services, 2000.

Sherman, L. (Ed.). *Misleading Evidence and Evidence-led Policy: Making Social Science More Experimental*, Annals of The American Academy of Political and Social Sciences, Vol. 589, 2003.

Sloan-Howitt, M. and G.L. Kelling, Subway Grafitti in New York City: "Gettin up" vs "Meanin it and cleanin it". In: R.V. Clarke (Ed.), *Situational Crime Prevention Successful Case Studies*. New York: Harrow and Heston, 1992.

Tilley, N. and A. Ford, *Forensic Science and Crime Investigation*, Crime Detection and Prevention Series, Paper 73. London: Home Office, 1996.

Van Kesteren, J.N., P. Mayhew and P. Nieuwbeerta, *Criminal Victimisation in Seventeen Industrialised Countries: Key-Findings from the 2000 International Crime Victims Survey*. The Hague: Ministry of Justice, WODC, 2000.

Von Hirsch, A., D. Garland and A. Wakefield (Eds), *Ethical and Social Perspectives on Situational Crime Prevention*. Oxford: Hart Publishing, 2000.

Wallerstein, J.S. and C.J. Wyle, Our law-abiding law breakers. *Probation*, 25, pp. 107–112, quoted in Gabor, T. (1994). *Everybody Does It: Crime by the Public*. Toronto: University of Toronto Press, 1947.

CHAPTER 6

THREATS TO THE NET: TRENDS AND LAW ENFORCEMENT RESPONSES

Christopher Painter *

INTRODUCTION

Since the beginning of civilization, criminals and law enforcement have battled to outwit, out-equip, and out-manoeuvre each other. The advent of the internet and computer networks in general has elevated this battle to new heights: allowing new methods to track criminal conduct, but also creating new types of crime and significant challenges to law enforcement investigations.

It is axiomatic that the internet has expanded dramatically over the last decade, growing at an exponential rate that often defies solid statistical analysis.[1] As multipurpose tools, these expanding computer networks facilitate business, communication, entertainment, and governmental goals. While the vast majority of people use computer networks to enhance the overall benefits to the world's inhabitants, a relatively small, but alarming percentage of users seek a darker side, employing this new and expanding technology to perpetrate criminal acts. This criminal conduct includes not only many traditional crimes being committed over a new and powerful medium – so called "old wine in new bottles" – like fraud, extortion and the distribution of child pornography, but also includes new crimes such as hacking, computer viruses, and distributed denial of service attacks, where the computer itself is the target of the crime. The exact scope of this problem, particularly in the case of computer network intrusions, is difficult to ascertain. Reliable statistics of computer network attacks are scarce and there is a serious under-reporting problem occasioned by corporate victims fearing adverse publicity or disruption to the continuity of their operations if they report incidents to law enforcement. Even with an incomplete statistical picture, however, society's increasing dependence on computers and computer networks elevates the significance of attacks on and disruptions of those systems and the importance of

---

*   The views expressed in this essay are those of the author and do not necessarily represent the views of the United States.

1   See generally, "The Big Picture: Traffic Patterns" on http://cyberatlas.internet.com/big_picture/ traffic_patterns.

Ernesto U. Savona (ed.), Crime and Technology: New Frontiers for Regulations, Law Enforcement and Research, 69–78.

effective investigation of and deterrence of those individuals who would attack them. Moreover, since computers are now used to control vital infrastructures, such as power grids, telecommunications, water and other vital systems, the consequences of computer crime take on a dimension beyond simple economic loss.

Against this backdrop, computer technology has changed the dynamics and character of crime. Computer networks allow wrongdoers to reach a vastly larger victim pool and create far more damage than they could in the physical world. They can do this with only modest resources and can cloak themselves in seeming anonymity. Indeed, this seeming anonymity, coupled with the easy availability of sophisticated hacking tools, emboldens those who might not commit criminal conduct in the physical world to wreak havoc in the virtual one. Though the motivation of hackers is beginning to become more financial, many still believe that breaking into someone else's system is justified by their curiosity. Furthermore, unlike traditional crimes that usually have a defined physical locus, computer crimes, whatever their motivation, can lack jurisdictional boundaries either by their nature or design – often crossing international boundaries even when the victim and attacker are located in the same country.

The changing nature of the crime problem, global connectivity, and other advances in technology, have created a number of unique challenges for law enforcement. Attributing criminal conduct on the web can be very difficult because of the technical and ephemeral nature of the evidentiary trail. This is complicated by the international nature of many of these investigations. Following the evidentiary trail through several different countries requires the data to still exist in those jurisdictions. Swift and sure international cooperation is required or the trail will quickly go cold. Moreover, assuming an attacker is located, the legal regime must proscribe his conduct or there will be no consequences for or deterrence of these destructive acts.

This essay discusses some of the challenges faced in computer crime investigations and conclude with some of the domestic and international efforts to deal with these challenges.

THE THREAT

Although the rise in traditional crimes being committed over the internet is often visible and to some degree ascertainable, measuring the scope of computer network attacks is very difficult. Although many widespread viruses and worms are well publicized, other computer intrusions seldom come to light and evidence of them is often anecdotal. Exact statistics on computer crime are elusive for two main reasons: under-detection and under-reporting.

First, only a small percentage of victims realize they have been victimized. Network and computer owners neglect intrusion detection systems and virus profiles updates. They overlook patches and remedies to reported vulnerabilities. Often the issue is one of resources rather than initiative. However, even in sectors with excellent resources, the lack of internal incident reporting procedures can still prevent the proper level of oversight for an incident to reach the ears of an individual empowered to act.

Even when entities overcome the detection difficulties, under-reporting is still an issue for a number of reasons. A common perception is that law enforcement cannot undertake a criminal investigation in a discrete manner that will protect the victim's stakeholders, whether private citizens, bank customers, or shareholders. Many victims fear the negative publicity that could trigger a loss in market share, customer confidence, or civil legal action.

Under-detection and under-reporting are the leading causes of misperceptions of computer crime. Some victims believe the cost/benefit analysis of the intrusions or incidents supports a continued stream of minor losses. The cost associated with restoration of service and remediation, or the downtime associated with removing an e-commerce server from operation are simply too great, given the level of threat or the minor financial loss in any given case. Acknowledging the above rationale for under-detection and under-reporting, the statistics available within the United States are still remarkable. The 2004 Computer Crime and Security Survey conducted jointly by the Computer Security Institute (CSI) and the Federal Bureau of Investigation (FBI) (CSI/FBI, 2004) includes an array of sectors including respondents from local, state, and federal government; high technology, education, retail, and manufacturing companies; legal organizations; and infrastructure such as utility, transportation, medical, financial, and telecommunications sectors. The results of the 2004 survey paint a serious, but not bleak, picture. 53% of the 481 computer security respondents reported some type of unauthorized use of their systems in 2004, less than the percentage reported over the last seven years (CSI/FBI, 2004: 8), causing just over US$140 million in financial losses (CSI/FBI, 2004: 10). However, only a small percentage of the respondents ever reported these incidents to law enforcement (CSI/FBI, 2004: 13). These results represent only a small fraction of U.S. victims and the survey does not claim to be a scientific sampling. Other measuring efforts are being conceived both in the U.S. and around the world to determine the scope and growth of this problem (National Hi-Tech Crime Unit, 2002). The facts behind the unauthorized use statistics are the focus of multiple efforts within the United States and elsewhere to increase detection, encourage reporting, and respond to the threats posed by the violators – both domestically and internationally.

Aside from the reporting issues, both computer facilitated crimes and computer network attacks illustrate some changes in the character of criminal conduct occasioned by cyberspace. First, the barriers to entry are low and the scope of potential damage is heightened. Computer network abuse depends more upon skill than resources. Where once a criminal enterprise may have required a costly physical investment, like a fancy front office for a fraudulent investment scheme, now one individual on one computer can perpetuate the same scheme through a website that can be erected in hours at practically no cost and reach thousands of victims around the globe. Moreover, with respect to computer network attacks, the nature of the threat is asymmetric. A single computer user can unleash a computer attack, such as many of the computer viruses and worms that have recently been in the headlines, and cause widespread and significant losses. In many of these instances, technical sophistication is no longer required. Hacking tools and malicious code are readily available on the internet. As the "I love you" virus[2] and February 2000 distributed denial of

2   The examples of computer network attacks are numerous and often garner a great deal of publicity. In the "I love you" virus, machines worldwide were compromised in hours. Though the investigation

service attack illustrate,[3] even a novice or teenager can, if so inclined, cause a good deal of damage.

This threat is exacerbated by the seeming anonymity that the internet offers. Individuals who may not risk attempting a physical world crime are emboldened to commit crimes over computer networks because they can easily obscure their identity. It also appears that many computer criminals do not fully appreciate the illegality and consequences of their acts. Most children understand that it is wrong to physically break into their neighbour's house, but many don't see the problem in breaking into their neighbour's computer. The motivation of attackers is also difficult to discern. Those who engage in hacking often assert that they were just satisfying their intellectual curiosity. Of course, to the victim, the motivation of the attacker is largely irrelevant – if someone breaks into your system, steals or destroys your information and compromises your privacy it does not matter that they were doing so to satisfy their curiosity or for monetary gain. In any event, with ever greater frequency, as the extortion cases above illustrate, hackers are committing their crimes not only to cause damage, but for financial reasons as well. In this sense, the two categories of computer facilitated crimes and crimes where the computer is the target begin to merge. Hackers combine their computer network attacks with extortion or other more traditional fraudulent conduct and traditional criminals are using the methods of sophisticated hackers to conceal their identity.

Many of these observations take on a new dimension given the global nature of the problem. Network criminals are further emboldened by the perception that they can escape apprehension when they are operating in the international arena. For example, a smart hacker located in Germany and attacking a computer in Germany may route his attack through computer systems in several different countries to evade capture. The reach of criminal conduct is also greatly enhanced. By the nature of the global internet, a hacker located anywhere in the world can launch an attack on, or steal information from, a computer located in any country, again with very little investment or resources.

---

quickly focused on a Philippine individual based on a analysis of the malicious code, the Philippines, at that time, had no law criminalizing this conduct.

3   In February 2000, a computer attack called a distributed denial of service attack was launched against many of the best known internet commerce sites in the United States including Yahoo!, Ebay, CNN and E*Trade. This kind of attack involves intruding into thousands of computers, converting those computers into "slave" or "zombie" computers that will do the bidding of the person controlling the network, and then causing those slaves to send information to a target computer on the internet at the same time so as to essentially knock it off the net or make it unavailable. Because people in the United States at that time were increasingly using these internet sites for commerce and communication this attack was a wake-up call in terms of the potential seriousness of computer crime. It was also a wake-up call in terms of the nature of the threat and the need for international cooperation. The investigation led back to Canada and was only successful due to the close cooperation of Canadian and U.S. authorities. The culprit turned out to be a fourteen-year-old boy with the computer moniker "mafiaboy" who did not himself possess a great deal of skill, but used tools developed by others to wreak substantial havoc.

CHALLENGES FOR LAW ENFORCEMENT

The spread of computer crime, the highly technical nature of investigations over computer networks and the ever present international nature of these cases all pose significant challenges for law enforcement. These challenges include having the technical expertise to conduct a network investigation, the availability of and legal access to relevant evidence, the ability to cooperate to investigate conduct that crosses international borders and the ability to punish conduct once the wrongdoer is found. Some of these challenges are practical, some legal and some technical.

In any case, the primary investigative step is to locate the attackers' origin. Attributing the conduct to a human being is the most difficult aspect of any computer investigation, but it is also the most critical. Without a suspect, investigations quickly falter. Although computer networks may give investigators new sources of evidence, like computer logs and access records, attribution is quickly complicated by the nature of our global communications capability. Any nefarious communication can transit multiple telecommunications carriers, providing different types of services, in different countries, with different data preservation policies, and data acquisition laws. Additionally, the provider, when served with proper, timely, adequate legal process, must respond positively to the evidence request – without alerting the target.

For example, assume an intrusion into the air traffic control system in country A that appears to originate from country B, but, in reality, came from a hacker in country C. Conducting an effective investigation is dependant on numerous factors. First, country A must have trained investigators who can understand the evidentiary trail – a capacity issue. Second, the relevant computer logs must exist in the first instance. This is a practical and legal issue. Whether the evidence exists could depend on the data protection laws of any of the counties in the chain. In some countries, service providers must destroy or anonymize data that is not necessary for billing. If the evidence is destroyed, the trail goes cold. Moreover, there are technical hurdles. Though computer logs can leave an electronic trail for law enforcement to follow in some cases, sophisticated hackers can hide or erase their trails or use other methods to evade detection. For example, the individual who perpetrated the PairGain stock fraud – the first internet-facilitated stock fraud in the U.S. – was captured in a little over a week because a highly trained investigator was able to follow a clear digital trail (Painter, 2001).[4] By contrast, it took over two years to apprehend notorious hacker

---

4   In an internet auction fraud case, users of internet bulletin boards hosted by Yahoo! Finance and other companies devoted to the discussion of a company named PairGain saw a message from an individual reporting that an Israeli company would purchase PairGain, a telecommunications equipment company located in California, for 1.35 billion dollars. The message contained a link to what it stated was the Bloomberg News story reporting the impending merger. Other messages, purportedly from other individuals, also discussed the news in excited terms advocating that readers purchase the stock immediately. When users clicked on the link in the first message they were taken to what appeared to be a legitimate Bloomberg News web page containing a detailed story on the merger. Although the page looked exactly like a real Bloomberg page – even to the point of including other links that took the reader back to the real Bloomberg service – it was, in fact, bogus and the story of the merger was false.

Kevin Mitnick who used hacker tools, cloned cell phones and multiple connections to hide his identity,[5] and many others are still at large. As technology advances, law enforcement will always be challenged to keep up with criminals who abuse that technology. Even if the evidence exists it may exist only fleetingly. Accordingly, investigators must react with much greater speed than in typical cases or the evidence will be lost. This is complicated as the number of hops in the chain increases. At every hop the possibility that the evidence will have disappeared threatens an investigation. This is exacerbated when the conduct crosses international boundaries. In each new country investigative capacity, legal ability and speed are paramount.

Third, investigators must have the legal capability to trace criminal conduct over systems in their own jurisdiction. The ability to conduct "trap and traces" of network attacks in real time may be paramount to finding an attacker. Moreover, the ability to obtain and preserve historical traffic and other data from communications carriers is often vital to determining the source of an attack. Again, the ability to do this, and do it in an expedited manner, is vital and becomes more complicated as additional jurisdictions are implicated. Fourth, there must be close and timely international cooperation. Investigators need to be able to cooperate and share appropriate information or the criminals will benefit. The necessity of such close cooperation is evident not only in this hypothetical but has been illustrated time and again. Finally, assuming the perpetrator is located and the evidence is sufficient, there must be a way to punish his or her conduct. All of the investigative capacity and legal tools in the world are useless if the actor can avoid accountability because a country has not yet modernized its laws to handle such conduct. Where countries lack substantive or procedural laws, or fail to have adequately trained investigators, they unwittingly create safe havens for computer criminals.[6]

Technical challenges posed by advancing technology and clever criminals will continue to be an issue regardless of the steps countries take but aggressive training and cooperation with the technical and communications industry can help alleviate these challenges. More than any other type of criminal conduct, investigation of computer crime requires an on-going dialogue with industry to keep abreast of new technology, educate them as to law enforcement needs and process, and overcome the reticence to report crime. In other respects, experience illustrates a way forward for countries around the globe.

In just two hours, the false news triggered a buying spree. PairGain stock rose over 31% on NASDAQ with ten times its normal volume. When the hoax was exposed the stock fell causing thousands of victims to lose substantial amounts of money. Although this was a traditional type of crime, the internet allowed it to be committed in a new and previously impossible manner. The physical world equivalent, perhaps printing tens of thousands of false newspapers, would be both impractical and ineffective. Similar schemes with various new twists have surfaced repeatedly both in the United States and around the world.

5   See U.S. Department of Justice press release regarding *U.S. v. Mitnick*, at http://www.cybercrime.gov/mitnick.htm. Infamous computer hacker Kevin Mitnick broke into the systems of dozens of companies around the world multiple times during a two-and-a-half-year hacking spree and, among other things, stole millions of dollars in proprietary source code.

6   Although the hypothetical posits a computer intrusion, many if not all of the same considerations would apply to the investigation of any illegal conduct on the internet or other computer networks.

ENHANCING THE WORLD'S ABILITY TO RESPOND TO COMPUTER CRIME

Many in the international community have recognized the pressing need to deal with the challenges of computer crime. The United States and many other countries over the last decade have revised their substantive and procedural laws and created trained cyber investigative units. In the United States and several other countries the effort has been expanded to train prosecutors and judges as well in these new crimes and investigations. Several international organizations have also undertaken substantial activities. In 1997, the G8 countries issued a set of ten Principles and a ten point Action Plan to deal with the challenges of high-tech crime and created a standing sub-group of the Lyon Group on Transnational Crime to specifically consider computer crime. These Principles and Action Plan formed the basis of two United Nations General Assembly Resolutions (United Nations, 2001; United Nations, 2004) and put forth basic tenets like the need for substantive and procedural laws and the need for cross-border cooperation.[7]

The High-Tech Crime Subgroup has met regularly since its creation and has created a 24/7 Network of computer crime investigators to preserve evidence and cooperate in emergency investigations that now boasts 40 members. The Subgroup has also propounded basic forensic principles; principles relating to cross-border investigations; recommendations for tracing transborder terrorist and other communications; created a checklist for data preservation and drafted principles relating to data availability;[8] held three joint law enforcement/industry conferences to enhance cooperation with the private sector; issued principles on protecting critical information

---

7   See, www.cybercrime.gov/intl.html#vc6, the Principles are:

1. There must be no safe havens for those who abuse information technologies.
2. Investigation and prosecution of international high-tech crimes must be coordinated among all concerned states, regardless of where harm has occurred.
3. Law enforcement personnel must be trained and equipped to address high-tech crimes.
4. Legal systems must protect the confidentiality, integrity, and availability of data and systems from unauthorized impairment and ensure that serious abuse is penalized.
5. Legal systems should permit the preservation of and quick access to electronic data, which are often critical to the successful investigation of crime.
6. Mutual assistance regimes must ensure the timely gathering and exchange of evidence in cases involving international high-tech crime.
7. Transborder electronic access by law enforcement to publicly available (open source) information does not require authorization from the state where the data resides.
8. Forensic standards for retrieving and authenticating electronic data for use in criminal investigations and prosecutions must be developed and employed.
9. To the extent practicable, information and telecommunications systems should be designed to help prevent and detect network abuse, and should also facilitate the tracing of criminals and the collection of evidence.
10. Work in this area should be coordinated with the work of other relevant international fora to ensure against duplication of efforts.

8   See G8 High-Tech Crime Subgroup documents, available at http://www.usdoj.gov/ag/events/g82004/index.html.

infrastructures; and created best practices for network security with regard to law enforcement. Interpol has created a number of regional "working parties" to deal with high-tech crime issues. A number of law enforcement individuals and groups have set up an International Cybercrime Training Action Group to better coordinate high-tech crime training. The Organization of American States and the Asia Pacific Economic Cooperation fora have each adopted cyber security strategies that promote stronger laws and capabilities. The European Union, the OECD (OECD, 2002), and other international organizations have also been active. This list is not meant to be exclusive, but instead is illustrative of the international recognition that is accorded to computer crime and the progress that is already being made.

Perhaps most significant among international activities is the work done under the auspices of the Council of Europe that resulted in the Convention on Cybercrime. The Convention requires countries to criminalize certain behaviours, including computer intrusion and damage, requires signatory nations to enact law enforcement procedural tools that allow for effective criminal investigation of cyber offences, and facilitates that expedited legal assistance in the ever-increasing number of international requests involving perishable computer data (Council of Europe, 2001). The contents of the Convention have already been presented in detail in the contribution by Fausto Pocar in this book. It is here worth being noted that the Convention serves as a model for developing a robust computer crime-fighting program. It is flexible enough to allow countries with very different legal systems to achieve the same ends. Both the civil and common law legal traditions were represented by countries participating in the drafting of the Convention, which used a goals-oriented focus to allow each signatory country the latitude to adapt the precise implementation of the Convention's articles to its particular legal system.

Any country can implement legislation or practices that fit within the Convention's stated goals. Such actions would benefit the entire international community, as well as the individual country and its neighbours. Moreover, whether by adoption or emulation, the Convention allows countries to start acting now, devoting their resources to meeting a current need rather than expending valuable time, energy and resources to pursuing another possibly duplicative or inconsistent global legal instrument. These efforts, coupled with increased training and cooperation, will help make our response more effective and enhance the protection of all of our citizens.

CONCLUSION

Computer crime is growing and poses significant challenges for law enforcement both domestically and internationally. In order to meet those challenges, we must recognize the necessity of three fundamental elements in each country: international cooperation; the need for countries and other regional groups to adopt substantive and procedural legal regimes criminalizing such conduct and facilitating the investigation of such crimes; and the need for individual countries to build capacity to investigate these new crimes. Much of the foundation already exists. We now should leverage those activities, including operational activities like the 24/7 Network and legal frameworks like that set out in the Convention on Cybercrime, to counter the mounting threat. Each day is a race to stay ahead of criminals and we are all dependant on each other to investigate and make sure this new breed of wrongdoers faces appropriate consequences. We cannot afford to wait.

REFERENCES

Council of Europe, *Convention on Cyber-Crime,* Budapest. 23 November, 2001.

CSI/FBI, *2004 CSI/FBI Computer Crime and Security Survey Ann. Rep. 9,* 2004.

National Hi-Tech Crime Unit, *Hi-Tech Crime – The Impact on U.K. Businesses,* 2002. [available at www.nhtcu.org under the Downloads section].

OECD, *OECD Guidelines for the Security of Information Systems and Networks: Towards a Culture of Security.* Paris: OECD, 2002. [available at http://www.ftc.gov/bcp/conline/edcams/infosecurity/popups/OECD_guidelines.pdf].

Painter, C., Tracing in Internet Fraud Cases: PairGain and NEI Webworld. *United States Attorneys' Bulletin.* May 2001. [available at http://www.cybercrime.gov/usamay2001_3. htm].

United Nations, *G.A. Res. 55/63, 55th Sess., U.N. Doc. A/RES/55/63,* 2001.

United Nations, *G.A. Res. 58/199, 58th Sess., U.N. Doc. A/RES/48/199,* 2004.

CHAPTER 7

PRIVACY AND INVESTIGATIVE NEEDS: PROGRESSING FROM INCOMPATIBLE TO COMPLEMENTARY POSITIONS

Giuseppe Busia

INTRODUCTION

All too frequently, security and the protection of human rights are presented as alternatives, being considered as mutually incompatible and therefore mutually exclusive objectives. Such a schematic proposition, however, is not one with which one can agree, since in a system calling itself democratic, the exigencies of security must necessarily be reconciled to the demands of basic human rights. As a result, one must advance from the idea of contrasting standpoints to an essential and incontrovertible where each such element complements the other.

Therefore it is in this light that one will endeavour to underline how, in particular, such an objective can (and must) be pursued with full respect for that detailed and intricate complex of rights which has now come to be grouped under the general umbrella of the protection of personal data.

The same rights, as well as being safeguarded as a Constitutional asset under Italian domestic law (as the Constitutional Court has regularly confirmed) have also been hallowed in the European Union in its Charter of Basic Human Rights (Arts. 7 and 8). Above all, these rights serve to categorise our system as a democratic one, helping us to avoid the pitfall of believing that everything that it is possible to do will thereby become both lawful and morally acceptable.

In the following pages, after taking a look at the risks to the individual arising form the acquisition of personal data and the employment of new technologies, we will indicate some of the limits inherent in the idea that the collation of more information will necessarily assist investigative activity. We will thus refer to the principal juridical safeguards contained in the legal regulations on personal data, especially in the limits prescribed for their handling for the purposes of the police authorities, and we will look in particular at certain specific categories of information utilised in the course of investigations. Finally, we will examine international experiences in the field of co-operation in the interests of security, which may be recognised as a valid instance of how it can be possible to balance and reconcile the needs of security and the needs to safeguard fundamental human rights.

Ernesto U. Savona (ed.), Crime and Technology: New Frontiers for Regulations, Law Enforcement and Research, 79–90.
© 2004 *Springer. Printed in The Netherlands.*

OBLIVION AS A RIGHT TO LIBERTY

In this connection, it is often necessary to recognise that whenever data on an individual is acquired and stored, even with the best possible and incontrovertible intentions, such as the prevention of crime and the preservation of security, this sphere of liberty is to some extent inevitably infringed. Indeed, if one knows something about another person, the possibility is lost of such information falling into oblivion, even if, for example, that person has changed profession, mode of life, attitudes, habits, ideas, etc: he loses the possibility of hiding it, even when he is intent on reconstructing his own identity on the basis of a new and different personality (the right to anonymity). In consequence, he loses some part of his freedom of personal choice and self-determination.

Being a prisoner of one's past means losing hope of ever changing or improving oneself: one thinks of the prostitute – I refer to actual cases without of course giving real names – who, having freed herself of those exploiting her, began to work in the world of show-business and achieved a certain reputation there, yet all the time had her past thrown in her teeth as an obstacle to her career advancement. And it is the same for so many women with similar experiences, for whom the past simply represents an obstacle to making a new life for themselves out of the limelight, building a family and re-establishing an identity so as to forget and cause to be forgotten a less happy phase of their existence.

One thinks also of those who have committed crimes, then paid their debt to society, reintegrated themselves in the world of employment and genuinely wish – as society has the duty to wish and to encourage – not to meet great impediments in their progress as a result of continuing reminders of their past. In the face of such cases, one has to ask how much the, albeit necessary, conservation and accessibility of their criminal record can assist the attainment of the aim of the fine provision in the Constitution – one of its most attractive ones because it is full of optimism for the individual – whereby the sentence served by the wrongdoer should look to his useful re-education (Art.27).

Often, as a result of the traces that we leave from an increasing use of electronic devices, we restrict our own freedom by putting others in a position to know more about us that we are able to anticipate. One thinks – relating once again an actual episode – of the young person participating in one of the many internet chat-shows who uttered, simply in jest and without real intent, certain political opinions. Well, some years later – after he had completed his studies and in all probably acquired different views – he had to undergo an interview for work in which his interviewer, after having examined his *curriculum vitae,* had the idea of consulting one of the many research engines on the Net in which he found the subject's electronic address and discovered the opinions that he had expressed so many years earlier. Leaving aside the question of the legitimacy of the interviewer's conduct, this episode shows how the conservation for a long period of personal information, perhaps even inadvertently, comes to represent a crucial element in the individual's life: simply because others have free access to such data; he is haunted by the ghosts of his past and so suffers a diminution of his personal liberty.

The legal system is not always able to make proper provision for such situations. Sometimes it gives just partial protection, being obliged to balance the yearning for anonymity with the other rights belonging to other individuals or society at large. However, it is incumbent upon everyone – beginning with those who work in the field of public security – to remember always that the mere conservation of personal information regarding an individual can have repercussions upon that person's life. So it should lay down that personal data should be gathered and retained only so far as pertinent, to the extent necessary and in accordance with the principles of proportionality – in other words, only so far as really vital for achieving aims that are appropriate and in cases where it is not possible to reach the same objective without resorting to personal data or by using less invasive techniques.

RISKS AND OPPORTUNITIES LINKED TO THE DEVELOPMENT OF NEW TECHNOLOGIES

Technological development increases exponentially the possibility of collecting and storing personal data regarding individuals. Indeed, there is a growth in the *number of data-banks* and their *inter-connexions,* both in the public and private sectors: one thinks, on the one hand, of the creation of a unified network in the field of public administration, which is surely opportune, in order to facilitate and enhance the quality of dealings with citizens, and on the other hand of the growing number of centralised private indices in which information is collected on the records of debtors and those seeking loans or extended credit.

At the same time there is an increased *memory capacity* for information in such electronic archives, enabling more and more personal data to be stored for ever longer periods of time. Together with the availability of increasingly rapid and sophisticated *research and indexing* facilities, this assists the identification of subjects and the revelation of ever greater information about them.

It is also becoming easier to gather personal data *without the subject being aware of this*: one only has to think of *cookies,* the small pieces of software which are downloaded on the user's equipment the moment he visits given pages on the web. Some of these are necessary to ensure a functional utilisation of the sites in question, but others collect a great deal on information on those surfing the net, with particular reference to the sites visited and thus to the tastes and interests of the people involved.

Finally, there is an increase in the *economic advantages* of collecting and handling data. The technologies have in fact made cheaper – and thus more widespread – certain forms of intrusion into the private lives of others: one only has to think of the phenomenon of "spamming", which has attained such dimensions as to prompt legislative intervention to contain it, even in countries like the United States, which hitherto had thought it possible to rely solely on the "invisible pressure" of market forces to deal with such problems.

All this inexorably brings about an increase in our vulnerability, not only with reference to the appearance of new offences, which are specifically based on the use of such technologies (one thinks of the so-called *computer crimes*) but – in the area which interests us – also with the widening diffusion of the so-called "identity thefts", tied to the fact that we are increasingly being represented not in terms of our true identity, but by identifying codes and signs transmitted on the electronic communication networks, which can be duplicated and used improperly by third persons to the detriment of the people to whom they refer or belong.

In general, therefore, we are witnessing a comprehensive increase in the risks tied to the improper use of data-banks, which inevitably reflects on investigative activities, both in regard to the use of various data-banks existing for the use of the police authorities and to the creation of electronic archives dedicated to security purposes and the repression of crime.

The unremitting advance of new technologies clearly presents an opportunity of which our society should take full advantage. The diffusion and constantly increasing use of them by the various categories of user, overall, is a symptom and consequence of the development, even in terms of democracy, of our society.

Yet, even in this case, it is always essential to recognise that, potentially at least, the more sophisticated such technologies become and – in parallel – the more useful they are in simplifying daily life, the more their utilisation leaves its electronic footprint: data showing when a given service has been used, for how long, for what reasons, in what location at which time, in inter-connection with what other subjects through the same instrument, etc.

The totality of such information, even when apparently detached and non-invasive, still reveals much about the relationships resorted to by an individual. If then, the data is stored for a long period – as is permitted at ever lower cost by these technologies – it becomes possible to construct the whole network of an individual's social relationships over a period of time, exceeding even the extent of which the subject himself is or can be aware.

These considerations also apply to those systems which purport to preserve the anonymity of the users, as with various services offered in the electronic communication networks. On the contrary, such services nearly always will permit the identity of the users to be discovered. This will happen unless one uses particularly cunning or sophisticated technologies, such as those employed by people with special reasons for remaining anonymous – perhaps because they are committing or intending to commit crimes.

LIMITATIONS TO THE CONCEPT THAT THE ACQUISITION OF MORE INFORMATION WILL NECESSARILY ASSIST INVESTIGATIONS

We now come to one of the paradoxes that we must confront, which supports ever larger collections of personal information for the purpose of preventing or repressing crime: in the very largest archives of information, data on all citizens come together ... including people with greater interest than others in not being included, because they are more concerned to avoid such inclusion, in particular those who have committed or intend to commit crimes.

Moreover, one must remember – as the organs responsible for protecting public security increasingly recognise – that indiscriminate acquisition of data, apart from being in excess of the desired objectives (and thus in violation of the principles set out above) do not always bring any advantage for the police. In fact, very often an excess of information imports a reduction in its quality and delays achieving success in the investigative operation, even when such indiscriminate collections do not hide deficiencies in the investigative process.

Finally, it is always necessary to consider that the collection and storage of data for long periods of time incurs very high costs, which – directly or indirectly – represent a burden on society, whether through the burdens imposed on businesses, which are passed on to the users, or through the costs charged to the public, which are ultimately borne by the taxpayers

What mostly interests us here, it that we must certainly accept that progress in technology creates important opportunities, with specific reference to their use for investigations, determining a quantitative and qualitative increase in the instruments available to operators in this field. Yet it has to be noted not only that such use must always conform to the limits imposed by law for the protection of personal data, but also that, simply because of its expansion, its efficacy may be reduced in achieving its objectives.

THE LEGISLATIVE RESPONSE REGARDING PERSONAL DATA AND THE DUTIES IMPOSED ON THE POLICE AUTHORITIES

These risks have been met by the regulations for the protection of data by a series of measures, which not only seek in general to prevent third parties from trespassing into the private life of individuals, according to the traditional concept of privacy, i.e. the right to be left alone. They also allow a decision on what use others may make of data concerning them, choosing not only whether a third party may have access to given items of personal information, but also the purposes for which it can be used, how long it can be stored, to whom it may be communicated, etc. The protection of data has become in this way a right of informational self-determination, gathering under its umbrella a growing number of rights, which, in the name of protecting the person and personal dignity, embrace and thereby enhance traditional rights, such as those of personal identity, and of the representation or freedom of manifestation of personal opinions.

The laws of the EU and Italy rest on certain fundamental forms of protection – referred to above – which are fully applied even in relation to the police authorities and more generally to everyone engaged in the maintenance of security. These are the principles of pertinence (the police may only gather and store data relevant to their investigations), necessity (data collected may not exceed what is necessary), reasonableness and due proportion between the objective and the mode of attaining it.

Further: since the police forces, unlike the rest of the community, are not obliged either to inform those interested of the fact that they are using data concerning them or to request their consent, and indeed are able to use personal information with many fewer restrictions (see Art.53 et seq. of the Code regarding the protection of personal data, Legislative Decree of 30th June 2003,No.196 and then the Privacy Code), it is essential that they adhere to the above-mentioned principles with particular rigour.

In fact, even the minor controls which any interested party may take over their operation – because, *inter alia*, of the permitted lack of notification and freedom from obtaining the consent of the subject – impose a particular "self-determination" in the grading of data to be obtained, in determining the periods of retention and in identifying individuals who may be subject to the totality of information from time to time considered necessary.

THE REGULATION OF SPECIFIC CATEGORIES OF PERSONAL DATA

Having set out the foregoing considerations of a general nature, we should now concentrate on the specific disciplines for certain types of personal data of special importance, which are often used by the forces charged with the maintenance of public security, so as to show how the principles enunciated have been operated in the particular regulation of various classes of data.

Electronic Traffic Data

Because of their intrinsic importance and the controversies regarding their regulation, we should begin with data concerning telephonic and electronic traffic. The Privacy Code, following the letter of Directive No.58 of 2002 to which it gives legal force, considers as traffic data "any data handled in transmitting a communication on an electronic network of communication or billing the same". Therefore, it provides a very broad definition, which derives from the most recent EU Regulations. These, recognising the growing convergence between instruments such as telephones, computers and televisions, have adopted a "technologically neutral" approach and – with the exception of certain details – tend to provide a common discipline for all electronic communications regardless of the terminal equipment used to effect them.

For this, data on electronic traffic includes not only telephony from fixed or mobile terminals (through which "calls" are achieved, i.e. the connections establishing bilateral communication in real time: see Art.4, para.2(b) of s.Igs.196/2003), but also other types of electronic communication, particularly fax, sms, mms. and e-mail.

Before describing the regulation of these, a basic clarification is needed: data on electronic traffic do not contain the content of conversations of messages, but only certain "external" information, such as the numbers or addresses of electronic mail, including the fact of the communication and the time it occurs. So then, it will be asked: what is the risk in the acquisition and storage of these? In reality, when one puts together information on the numbers called by an individual, it is possible to assemble a network of his personal and social relationships. By establishing the frequency and length of communications, and whether they occur at any time or merely during office hours, one can identify the type of relationship existing between the communicating parties.

For this reason, the Constitutional Court, well before the coming into force of the legal provisions on personal data, unequivocally recorded how "... the extent of the safeguard for communications contained in Art.15 of the Constitution ... comprises not only the secrecy of the content of the communication, but also the identity of the subjects and references to the time and place of the communication itself" (Decision No.18 of 1993).

For the same reason, as we have said, such information is regulated by a series of specific provisions, both in the EU Directives and in the Italian legislation giving effect to them. The Privacy Code provides in general terms, in fact, that data on electronic traffic must be cancelled or rendered anonymous when no longer necessary for the purposes of transmitting an electronic communication (Art.123). However, the provider of services is authorised to handle information that is strictly necessary for invoicing and payments for a period not exceeding six months, excepting the further specific retention that is required for court proceedings. A further handling is also permitted to the extent and for the period necessary for promoting electronic communication services or providing added value services, but this is subject to the consent of the subscriber and user, which may be withdrawn at any time. All this is also covered by specific safeguards concerning both the information to be given to the interested parties and certain limitations to the access to such information on the part of people working for the service provider.

Apart from the handling that is necessary under the terms of a contract, the Privacy Code laid down – and this is of particular interest – that only data relative to *telephonic* traffic (and so excluding all other communications on telecoms networks) may be retained by the provider for two and a half years for the purpose of discovering or repressing criminal activity within the terms of a Ministerial Decree adopted on a Declaration in accordance with the Authority (Art.132).

In the endeavour to broaden the scope of this last provision, which was considered too restrictive for the purposes of investigations, on the eve of the coming into force of the Privacy Code, the Government approved a Decree Law (No.354 of 2003) which provided an extension to five years of the permitted retention of data on telephonic traffic and a similar extension of the same rules relating to internet communications, as well as a suspension – until 2006 – of the former regulations (Decree Law No.171 of 1998) which should in fact have ceased to operate last January. The effect of this, in fact, is to reduce significantly the safeguards of every citizen's liberty, albeit for the laudable purpose of repressing crime.

Such periods of permitted retention of data were notably greater than those in effect in other European countries, which, however, only had to face up to the terrorism emergency after 2001 and encountered major opposition to the introduction of even much shorter periods. This was due not only to the resistance among the organizations protecting civil rights, but more generally to all those who were accustomed to relying on legal provisions such as those protecting privacy in the European Union's Charter of Basic Human Rights (see the cited Arts.7 and 8).

Fortunately, however, after a mobilization of institutions and citizens, the Italian Parliament did a significant about-face. So, the Law converting the Decree re-limited the scope of applicability of Art.132 of the Privacy Code to telephonic traffic, laying down an initial permitted period of retention of two years (rather than the two and a half years in the emergency provision). After that period, the same information may be retained for a further two years (rather than a further two and a half years) only if this is for the repression of the crimes listed in Art.407, para. 2(a) of the Code of

Criminal Procedure (for which there is an extended period permitted for the continuation of investigations) as well as those damaging to informatics and telecoms systems.

By contrast with the original text of the Code, the emergency provision had provided a detailed description of the mode of acquiring data. And in this field also the converting Law has provided for the introduction of a series of modifications tending to offer greater safeguards, laying down in particular that only the court (and not even the Public Prosecutor) may order the acquisition of data requested by the authorities or by one of the parties. Moreover, after the first two years, the court may only authorise the acquisition if there is sufficient evidence of the crimes previously cited. Finally, the Italian Parliament has also decided to empower the Authority (rather than the Minister of Justice) to define – through a declaration under the terms of Art.17 of the Privacy Code – the measures and devices to safeguard the interested party, so extending the guarantees for the protection of personal privacy.

Data on Location

Among the most sensitive and overall most valuable information for police investigations, emphasis must be laid on data concerning the location, or information indicating the geographic site, of the terminal equipment of the user of an electronic communication service. This permits not only locating with great precision the subject, his map reference, altitude and direction of movement, but at the same time can help construct an important image of the subject's personality. The handling of such data is generally connected to the provision of the so-called "added value" services, such as the description of the neighbourhood, the indication of where commercial forces of a given category that are being sought are to be found or the remote control of vehicles, animals or persons.

Services are becoming more available which permit the location of third parties other than those making the request for information: indeed there are commercial services aimed at locating everyone who has a mobile telephone number, provided that the terminal is kept open and is recorded in a relevant list. Such a list could be a group of friends or a family (within which such treatment could create very delicate problems, notwithstanding the safeguards contained in the Law, to which we will briefly allude). But what is not excluded may slip through into forms of control of employees by an employer, despite the prohibitions concerning the remote control of workers.

To give an idea of the rapid spread of such services, it suffices to mention that, until a few months ago, there was a heated debate on the legitimacy of the use of "electronic bracelets" to control the movements of prisoners released on probation. Last Summer a very similar device was used on beaches by mothers fearful that the children might stray too far. ...

It seems well established that the knowledge of such information makes it possible to reconstruct precisely the various actions taken (one thinks of questions as to the nearest petrol station or restaurant) or the interests (every time information is requested as to the location of something) of the person who has utilised or been the object of the service, to the point of constructing a personality profile of that person. Moreover, it is clear that the knowledge of such facts becomes even more important – and hence threatening to the persons concerned – the longer they are stored, even if the aim is the apparently useful one of better personalising the service offered; indeed this is exactly the logic of added value services.

Because of the specific risks connected to their handling, the Privacy Code, consistent with the intent of Directive No.58 of 2002, devotes to such data a specific discipline in relation to information on electronic traffic, which we have already examined in some detail. More particularly, data on location may be handled only if made anonymous or with the prior consent of the user or subscriber, (which may be revoked at any time) and to the extent and for the period necessary for the provision of the requested added value service. Even after the grant of such consent, the user and subscriber retain the right to request, free of charge and by a simple procedure, the temporary interruption of the handling of such data for each connection to the Net or for each transmission of communications (Art.126).

The provider of the service, before requesting consent, is also required to inform the interested parties as to the nature of the data to be handled, on the aims and on the duration of such handling, as well as on the possibility that data may be transmitted to a third party for the provision of added value services.

Finally, as a further precaution, the Privacy Code has laid down that the handling of such information may be permitted solely to those handling it under the direct authority of the provider of the electronic communication service, or, as the case may be, the provider of the Net or of the third party providing the added value service. In every case, the handling must be limited to what is strictly necessary for the provision of the service and must ensure the identification of the person responsible who has access to the data including such access through an operation of automated interrogation.

Video-Surveillance and Biometric Analysis

Particular importance for police activities attaches to personal information accessible from video-surveillance installations, the growing use of which for the protection of persons or property, despite being often justified in the interests of security, still represents an increasing intrusion into individual privacy.

Indeed, with growing frequency, such systems come to be combined in various ways with sophisticated instruments which will ensure the identification of persons through "biometric analysis" (geometry of the face, irises, etc.) which enables the newly acquired information to be compared with previously memorised data.

No one doubts the usefulness and sometimes the indispensability of the use of such technologies in supporting the security of citizens. Nevertheless, it is clear that even in this case too, it is necessary to ensure a proper balance between such exigencies and those linked to respect for the fundamental rights of people, who must not be condemned to live under the perpetual surveillance of others, even if such an operation may ultimately be of benefit to them.

The organs charged with protecting personal data have spoken a number of times about such problems, both in the Council of Europe and the European Union. The

Italian Authority also, as well as setting out a ten-point pronouncement on the use of such instruments, has had cause to intervene innumerable times to prevent excessive on non-consented data use. In this case also, the guideline principles are those mentioned above: relevance, non-excess and proportionality, which prohibit the generalised collection of personal information which is not justified by situations posing a concrete risk tied to objective circumstances.

These are principles which should govern not only the phase of information-collection (for example, avoiding the installation of an excessive number of video-cameras, giving access to them up only when really necessary, adjusting their catchment-area in such a way as not to collect excessive data, etc.), but also – and this is surely the most important element for investigative applications – the subsequent phases of data-storage.

In this regard, there is the rule under which the data collected must be erased as soon as it is no longer needed to meet its purposes, while access to it may in certain cases only be sanctioned for the police authorities where a criminal act has been confirmed. All this prevents the ever increasing number of video-camera installations leading to the systematic storage of data secured over time, which is permitted only if justified to provide evidence on given events. This is the case even though recognition of the usefulness of such records may support and in practice has supported investigations into a variety of crimes.

With specific reference to video-cameras, it should finally be mentioned that the materials will be more fully and organically systematised in a specific code of deontology and good practice "for the treatment of personal data obtained by electronic instruments for recording photographic images", which will need to lay down specific modes of handling and simplified forms of providing information to the subject-party in order to ensure the lawfulness and correctness of the operation (cf.Art.134, Privacy Code).

Genetic Data

The general principles described above are obviously more stringently applied in relation to particularly sensitive data, such as genetic data, being more and more often used for identification purposes in the course of police investigations. As part of data appropriate for revealing a state of health, genetic information is the most intimate, with a capability, *inter alia*, of incurring the risk of discrimination. This is so, not only when representing a permanent element immutable on the part of the subject, but also because information is contained directly which is not confined to the subject, but may concern also his relatives; and finally because not only past history is revealed, but also prospects for the future. Such is the case, for example, in techniques of "predictive medicine", capable of identifying possible delayed-onset illnesses and thus of providing an insight into the future which perhaps should not be known and certainly should not be disclosed.

Because of these characteristics of theirs, the handling of genetic data, no matter who has generated it, is only permitted in cases where the Authority has given specific consent with the knowledge of the Ministry of Health, and after obtaining the favourable opinion of the Senior Health Council. It has been further laid down that such an authorization must contain, *inter alia*, the indication of the elements to be recorded, with particular reference to the specification of the objectives pursued and the prospective consequences of unexpected information coming to light as a result of the handling of data as well as the right to subject data to the same treatment for legitimate purposes (Art.90, Privacy Code).

CONCLUSIONS

The international and domestic climate following the terrorist outrages of 11th September 2001 and subsequent tragic events up to the present day, have prompted every occidental state to adopt especially stringent measures in the field of public security.

Unfortunately, behind the emotive pressure of such events, some measures have been adopted which do not always respect the principles and criteria mentioned above: measures which too often fail to give due regard to the long-term consequences of such policies (see in this connection Opinion 10/2001, approved on 14th December 2001 by the Group of European Guarantees provided for in Art.29 of Directive No.95/44/EC).

It is probably true that such greater stringency has represented a partially inevitable response to the various emergency situations confronting governments and organs responsible for safeguarding their citizens' security. Nevertheless, even such extreme circumstances can never justify an excessive diminution of basic human rights.

This is because, when everything has been duly taken into account, such rights are also the mirror of the values which those threatening security aims to jeopardise and destroy.

CHAPTER 8

TECHNOLOGY AND INTELLIGENCE COLLECTION

Neil Bailey

INTRODUCTION

We have all witnessed tremendous advances in technology over the last 50 years, affecting our everyday lives, and in many cases making our lives easier. Technology does not discriminate between criminals and law abiding citizens – it is freely, and increasingly cheaply, available to all sectors of society. It is unfortunate that often criminals are the first to recognise the benefits of new technology, to embrace it and use it – law enforcement agencies then have to respond, and adopt counter measures.

Some crimes are made easier by the application of new technology, whilst others are totally dependent on it. A good example of this latter category is the transfer of paedophile material across the internet. As far as the former category is concerned, the application of new technology to assist criminal activities is extremely diverse. Over 30 years ago a significant problem was the smuggling of drugs, tobacco goods and illegal immigrants across the English Channel in small boats At that time, the smugglers needed to identify crew for the boat who were able to navigate using charts and a compass – without such knowledge, they were unlikely to reach their intended destination. Now, it is possible to purchase a small handheld Global Position Satellite System (GPS) that enables the most incompetent crew to navigate the Channel easily. A sophisticated handheld GPS with built in maps and navigation charts can be purchased in most chandlers or airport shops for about 200€ – easily within reach of all potential traffickers. We must obviously recognise the tremendous advances in the detection and prevention of crime that have taken place during this technological revolution. I am going to concentrate on how the law enforcement community should respond to the threat posed by the increasing availability of technology to criminals. We must identify, and exploit, opportunities for law enforcement that arise from the use of it, and if necessary, persuade governments to legislate to enable law enforcement to take advantage of those opportunities.

THE IMPACT OF BORDERLESS TECHNOLOGY ON LAW ENFORCEMENT

Firstly, we must accept that technology does not recognise geographic and political boundaries, and it is not realistic to restrict the availability of it. The growth of mobile

Ernesto U. Savona (ed.), Crime and Technology: New Frontiers for Regulations, Law Enforcement and Research, 91–96.
© 2004 *Springer. Printed in The Netherlands.*

(cellular) telephony over the last fifteen years is an example of how widely and rapidly new technology can become available.

The expansion in the use of the internet is equally dramatic. The internet has introduced new categories of crime – the transfer of paedophile material across countries, and indeed continents, being a prime example. The internet has increasingly become a medium for communication, via e-mails and chat rooms for example, and encryption is widely and cheaply available. If paedophile images are transferred and downloaded onto the hard disk of a PC, recipients will go to great lengths to 'hide' the images or encrypt them to prevent their discovery, either by other members of his family, or by law enforcement officials searching the machine. Detecting such crimes, and gathering evidence that can sustain a prosecution in such cases requires radically different skills to the traditional 'detective' skills of previous generations. It is essential that law enforcement agencies keep abreast of the latest technological advances – not just those appearing on the market now, but also those that will reach the market in future – it is vitally important to identify threats and opportunities at an early stage. There then needs to be an assessment of whether the advance is likely to prove attractive to criminals, and whether and when it is realistic to expect them to be able to obtain it. This initial research will often require co-operation with manufacturers and suppliers, and a thorough understanding of the technical issues involved. This has implications for recruitment policies in Law Enforcement Agencies – and I suggest that 'brigading' this expertise into dedicated units is the way forward.

THE EXPERIENCE OF THE NATIONAL HI-TEC UNIT IN UK

The United Kingdom established a National Hi-Tec Crime Unit (NHTCU) in 2001. That unit has defined two categories of 'Cybercrime':

1. "New crimes, new tools – new crimes committed against computers and IT networks which present new opportunities to criminals and new challenges to law enforcement agencies, for example hacking and viruses, denial of service attacks and 'spoof' websites" (spoof website = a website purporting to be that of a legitimate organisation, that often requests visitors to input personal details and passwords in order to commit fraud).
2. "Old crimes, new tools – traditional crimes supported by use of the internet and hi-technology, such as fraud, blackmail and extortion, paedophilia and pornography, identity theft and cyberstalking".

The remit of the NHTCU is as follows:
The NHTCU will:

• Support or lead activity against serious and organised hi-tec crime of a national or transnational nature
• Respond with an investigative capacity to all threats to the critical national infrastructure

- Undertake strategic assessments
- Develop intelligence
- Support and co-ordinate law enforcement operations
- Offer 'best advice' to law enforcement and business.

Of course the strategy adopted in the United Kingdom may not be applied precisely in all other jurisdictions, but the principle of establishing a multi-agency group of experts with a thorough and current understanding of new technology has to be the right way forward. Such units or 'clusters' of experts in different countries can establish formal and informal networks that ensure developments in one country are shared. The companies that manufacture and market new technology operate globally, and it is reasonable to assume that methods to counter the use of it by criminals can also be applied across geographic and jurisdictional boundaries.

Closer co-operation between Law Enforcement Agencies should ensure that where new technology poses a threat to current investigative techniques, that threat can be countered by governments introducing legislation to impose obligations on manufacturers and service providers. Such obligations cannot be imposed in isolation, as otherwise the manufacturers or service providers will transfer their operations to jurisdictions that have not introduced the appropriate legislation or regulatory regime. We must ensure that our response to manufacturers and service providers is consistent, reasonable, and proportionate. If we ensure that these criteria are met, it is far more likely that they will accept our pleas for legislation or regulation, and not lobby governments to oppose them.

Regulation or legislation should enable law enforcement agencies to be equally effective in whichever jurisdiction they are based, and should recognise the requirement for them to conduct investigations into offences that have been committed anywhere in the world.

By way of example, a paedophile resident in the UK may hold an account with an Internet Service Provider (ISP) in the USA, and he may access that account from his laptop in a Hotel room in Spain. When he transfers paedophile material from a site hosted in Thailand, the image passes through cyberspace, which clearly recognises no geographic boundaries, and utilises a telecommunications (telecoms) network that routes the call through the cheapest links in a complex chain. If the paedophile is subsequently apprehended whilst on holiday here in Courmayeur, the complexity of the investigation that then commences is immediately apparent. The investigator needs to know that wherever the cyber trail leads, the obligations of the Communication Service Providers (CSPs) and Internet Service Providers (ISPs) to co-operate will be broadly similar – there must be no safe havens for serious or organised criminals who use the internet for illicit activities. "Serious and organised criminals have always sought secure means of communicating with each other. E-mail, internet chat rooms and instant messenger services offer new options, as do web based and client server mail accounts, websites and message boards. These methods can be used to co-ordinate criminal activity, locate victims, and to make new criminal contacts, as well as to procure goods and services related to the criminal enterprise. They provide speed of communication and relative anonymity" (UK NCIS Threat Assessment, 2003).

"When combined with the communication systems and methods I have described, encryption tools offer a further level of security to serious and organised criminals in terms of the data they store and exchange. Encryption tools are readily available on the internet, and can be used both with data stored on hard disks and with communications such as e-mails. The indications are that organised criminals are increasingly using sophisticated and high-powered encryption tools to protect themselves."(UK NCIS Threat Assessment, 2003).

CONCLUSION

International co-operation and a thorough understanding of the technical and legal issues involved are vital if we are to be effective against these new threats. Whilst enhanced regional co-operation, for example co-ordination within the European Union through Europol, is a positive development, in respect of cyber crime political and geographic boundaries are irrelevant – and this must be understood by legislators as well as those tasked with investigating and prosecuting offences.

In the field of communications, the adoption of new technology has presented opportunities to obtain evidence previously unavailable – but often a balance has to be struck with the reasonable expectation of privacy in a free society. I can best illustrate this dilemma by returning to the subject of mobile cellular telephony. Criminals always have, and always will, need to communicate. Before the advent of digital mobile telephones, communications between a supplier or transporter of drugs and his recipient – who would often also be the organiser, would be made from anonymous payphones. Now of course, all those involved in a trafficking operation communicate by mobile telephone, and a record of the time and number dialled are available to the service provider. Before the advent of 'prepaid' or 'pay as you go' mobiles, this data was retained for billing purposes, but this is no longer required. The CSP still captures the data, but if it does not need to be kept for billing purposes, why should they retain it? If they do retain it, should they destroy it as soon as they no longer require the data for billing/business purposes? We know that the information contained within the databases held by CSPs can be vital in establishing association between criminals, and can make the crucial difference in securing a conviction, but this data is often required many months or years after it was captured. There is an obvious conflict of interest for the CSP – balancing the needs of law enforcement, and the benefits to society as a whole in convicting offenders, against the expectation of shareholders that the business will not spend money retaining data that is not required for business purposes. The expectations and rights of privacy under the European Convention on Human Rights also have to be considered, alongside the Data Protection provisions of International Conventions (e.g. Strasbourg) and national Data Protection legislation (e.g. The United Kingdom Data Protection Act).

This is a complex area, and again one in which international co-operation is essential – most CSPs are global organisations, operating in many countries and they have a reasonable expectation that regulation and legislation should be consistently applied in whichever market they are operating. The criminal will soon exploit those inconsistencies, which will benefit neither society as a whole nor shareholders in CSPs. A global economy has resulted in much greater collaboration amongst providers of goods and services, but I suggest that the collaboration amongst law enforcement agencies has not increased to the same extent, and if we are to confront and counter the advantages that criminals have derived from the 'technological revolution', that collaboration must be enhanced. This extends far beyond the world of telecommunications and the internet – airline computer systems are a good example. Records are maintained by the airlines for quite considerable periods – if you are a member of a 'Frequent Flyer' programme, a search of the airline database will reveal all sectors that you have flown for a year or more. Most people are aware that this data is collected, but would they be happy if law enforcement was given unregulated access to it? I suspect that amongst 'innocent travellers' the majority would not be concerned, believing that law enforcement would act responsibly, but a significant minority would disagree. Of course an airline could court popularity amongst criminals by declaring that records would be erased after the flight had landed safely; whilst this might please some, I suspect the majority would still be in favour of law enforcement accessing such records to support prosecutions for serious crime and terrorist offences.

This apparent conflict between privacy, profits and public duty can only be addressed by a series of partnerships – firstly at the national level between industry, law enforcement, legislators and regulators, and then at the international level. This second, international, level of partnership must recognise the reality of technological advances, and not restrict partnerships to countries grouped together by virtue of geography. United Nations bodies such as ISPAC can make an effective contribution to this.

REFERENCES

Adams, R., *The Mobile Phone Market.* (Technical Report) Analyst, Strategic Research & Development Unit, London, National Criminal Intelligence, 2003.

Dataquest Inc, *Worldwide Mobile Phone Sales Increase by 45%* (Statistics and Analysis, World News) USA, GSMBOX.co.uk, 2001.

Gartner Dataquest, *Worldwide Sales of Mobile Phones* (Statistics and Analysis, World News) UK, GSMBOX.co.uk, 2001.

Horne, G.A., *The New Europe in the World Economy,* International Chamber of Commerce, UK, International Systems and Communications Ltd, 2000.

NCIS, *The UK Threat Assessment, "The Threat from Serious and Organised Crime 2003"* (Technical Report) London, National Criminal Intelligence Service, 2003.

OFTEL, *Consumers' Use of Mobile Telephony Q8 February 2002* (Technical Report) London, Office of Telecommunications, 2002.

OFTEL, *Consumers' Use of Mobile Telephony Q14 August 2003* (Technical Report) London, Office of Telecommunications, 2003.

SRI Consulting, *Mobile Phones to Outnumber Wireline Phones by 2005* (Statistics and Analysis, World News), UK, GSMBOX.co.uk, 2000.

Strategis Group, *Mobile Handset Sales Reach 291 Million* (Statistics and Analysis, World News) UK, GSMBOX.co.uk, 2000.

CHAPTER 9

NEW CHALLENGES FOR RESEARCH: TECHNOLOGY, CRIMINOLOGY AND CRIME SCIENCE

Ronald V. Clarke

INTRODUCTION

Technology changes everything, crime included. The internet has created a completely new environment in which traditional crimes – fraud, identity theft and child pornography – can take new forms and prosper. Globalisation, partly the product of new technology, has opened up vast new opportunities for organized crimes such as money laundering, credit card forgery, trade in body parts and, of course, terrorism. Technology is also delivering new ways to control crime, including facial recognition software, global positioning devices, radio-frequency identification tags and many, many more.

This new environment of crime and crime control has radical implications for criminology. It is argued below that if the discipline is not to become sidelined and irrelevant criminologists must make changes that go far beyond a re-focusing of research topics. The changes (summarised in Table 1) must address criminology's mission, its theories and its methodologies with the collective result of making the discipline more directly relevant to crime control. The need for this has long been apparent and has only been made more obvious by advancing technology. This paper will suggest that if criminologists fail to act, universities may begin to create new departments of crime science (Laycock 2003), instead of building departments of criminology.

At the outset, it should be made clear that this is not a normal academic article in which facts and evidence are carefully assembled to support the argument. Rather, it expresses the view of one criminologist whose self-appointed mission has been to improve the scientific basis of crime policy. Having said that, it is probably congruent with the views of other criminologists who now regard themselves as crime scientists (see Laycock 2004; Pease 2001).

CHANGES IN MISSION

As a result of its origins in sociology, in law and in philosophy – all cerebral disciplines – criminology has defined itself as concerned principally with understanding and explaining crime. This scholarly role might have been defensible when crime was

Ernesto U. Savona (ed.), Crime and Technology: New Frontiers for Regulations,
Law Enforcement and Research, 97–104.
© 2004 *Springer. Printed in The Netherlands.*

TABLE 1. Differences of emphasis between criminology and crime science.

Criminology	Crime science
Mission	
Understand criminals	Understand crime
Long-term social reform	Immediate crime reduction
Help the criminal underdog	Reduce harm to victims
'Pure'	'Applied'
Theory-led	Problem-led
Shun policy	Embrace policy
Theory	
Distant causes paramount	Near causes paramount
Opportunity secondary	Opportunity central
Crime pathological	Crime normal
The WHY of crime	The HOW of crime
Criminal dispositions	Criminal choice
Criminal motivation	The rewards of crime
Anomie, subcultures and conflict theory	Routine activities, rational choice
Sociology, psychiatry, law	Economics, geography, biology, planning, computer science
Research methods	
Cohort studies	Crime patterns
Criminal careers	Hot spots
Regression analysis	Crime mapping
Self-reported delinquency	Victim surveys
Randomised control trials	Crime specific case studies
Long term studies in depth	Rapid appraisal techniques
Applications and audience	
Crime and delinquency in general	Specific crime and disorder problems
Sentencing/treatment/social prevention	Detection/deterrence/situational prevention
Social workers/probation officers	Police, planners and security industry
Social policymakers	Business and management
Scholarly treatises	Policy briefs
Careers in academia	Careers in prevention/security/police

mostly an irritant to society, and regarded as the inevitable result of psychological and social disadvantage. Indeed, understanding and explaining crime played an important part in fashioning a humane response to criminals. But crime in the form of terrorism is now a serious threat to society and merely seeking to explain and understand is to fiddle while Rome burns. Criminology's mission must be redefined so that it is firmly focused on helping to find ways of controlling crime, especially of these more serious kinds.

This means that criminologists must no longer imagine themselves engaged in 'pure' science (if ever that was realistic) and must embrace the role of 'applied' scientists. They must give up the idea that striving for policy relevance uniquely distorts the quest for a 'pure' understanding of crime. Pure objective understanding of crime is impossible because we can never be free of political, disciplinary or theoretical bias. Criminological theories are always provisional and incomplete and, because they are rarely subjected to the test of policy relevance, it is easy to be deceived about their value. Worse, persisting with the search for 'true,' full understanding is like the endless pursuit of the philosopher's stone and is a recipe for disappointment and frustration. Criminologists can avoid this fate by trying to make the discipline useful – and if this is to be done, certain things must follow.

Above all, criminologists must focus on the things that can be changed. Nearly 30 years ago, Wilson (1975) warned that if criminologists persisted in framing explanations of crime in terms of variables that cannot be changed they would be doomed to policy irrelevance. Referring to two prominent theories, he asked how society could ever abolish relative deprivation or how mothers could be made to love their children more consistently. Focussing on the distant causes of crime has indeed consigned criminologists to a policy vacuum: proposals for change are utopian in character; even if they could be made, it is unclear whether they would be effective; if they were to work, they could only deliver crime reductions in the distant future; and because of the passage of time it would be very difficult to determine whether they actually had worked. No hard-headed policy maker would expend political capital and commit economic resources in pursuit of such an uncertain agenda.

On the other hand, there are now dozens of studies showing that crime can be immediately, and sometimes dramatically reduced by focussing on near causes through the reduction of situational opportunities (Clarke 1997; Hough and Tilley 1998). Unfortunately, this approach does not sit easily with the social reformist ambitions of many criminologists. They believe that reducing crime by these means diverts people's attention from the more important goal of dealing with the inequities in society, whereas in truth crime should never have been hijacked by this political agenda. Others see opportunity reduction as simplistic and somehow beneath the grand scope of their vision. But these criminologists are blind to the very real intellectual challenges of devising effective ways to reduce opportunities that, at the same time, are ethically and socially responsible (Von Hirsch et al. 2000). The result is that criminology has failed to make the contribution to crime prevention and control that it could otherwise have done during at least the past 25 years when it has been apparent that opportunity reduction can deliver valuable reductions in crime.

CHANGES IN THEORY AND RESEARCH

In the criminology of the future, the disciplinary origins of a criminologist in law, psychology or sociology should no longer be the source of authority and status. Nor should these benefits be conferred by mastery of any particular theories – unless they assist the mission of controlling crime. This means that criminologists must be prepared to abandon theories that have been the mainstay of the discipline for decades. In particular, they must downgrade the importance of theories that define crime as the product of disadvantage. Because crime has continued to rise when income and other social indices have improved, these theories have lost credibility (Felson 1998). They certainly cannot explain crime on the internet, which is rarely committed by disadvantaged delinquents. More helpful to crime policy is the 'criminology of everyday life' (Garland 2001), including rational choice and routine activity theory (Clarke and Felson 1993). However, in devising effective policies, criminologists must seek the help of disciplines they have previously spurned, the most obvious of which are economics, biology, demography, geography and town planning. In an increasingly technological age, they could also be helped by scientists and engineers.

The belief that crime is the product of discrimination and disadvantage has had another unfortunate effect. It has led criminologists to align themselves habitually with the criminal underdog and ignore the harm he inflicts on victims and society. But they should not overlook what Taylor et al. (1973) pointed out more than 30 years ago. This was that discrimination and disadvantage do not propel robbers through the doors of the bank; instead robbers *choose* to rob banks because they want money, and they want large amounts of it. Instead of always sympathizing with the criminal's plight, criminologists should recognize that crime is fuelled by greed and selfishness as much as by any other cause. Instead of indulging in utopian schemes to improve the lot of the criminal, criminologists should be helping to find ways to tighten security and increase the risks of being caught so that people will no longer even contemplate robbing a bank. When surveying the literature on internet scams for our book on *Superhighway Robbery,* Graeme Newman and the present author were struck by the fact that criminological commentaries on the internet were preoccupied with the so-called 'exclusionary' effect on crime resulting from the fact that poorer people cannot afford computers. Most of these commentaries ignored that fact that the internet has opened up vast new opportunities for crime and failed to mention the urgent need to find ways of preventing this crime (Newman and Clarke 2003).

If criminologists were to focus more directly on prevention and control, this would profoundly affect research. First, there would be much less interest in explaining criminality – why certain individuals or groups become involved in crime – and more in explaining crime itself. Explaining crime involves much more than explaining criminal dispositions because its commission depends crucially also on the existence of opportunities for crime. Criminologists have tended to see opportunity as subsidiary to motivation, but the latest thinking and research sees motivation and opportunity as crucially interdependent. This interdependence exists at an immediate situational level – a camera left on the seat of an unlocked car can tempt someone to steal it – but more importantly it also operates at a systemic, societal level. The existence of many easy opportunities for crime draws people into committing crime. They become habituated to crime and always alert to criminal opportunities. If easy opportunities are curtailed, people will not always be on the lookout for ways to benefit themselves illegally (Felson and Clarke 1998).

Where prevention and control are the objectives, research will need to focus more on *how* crime is committed and less on *why* it is committed. Understanding the steps in the process of committing crime, and understanding the conditions that facilitate its commission, helps us see how we can intervene to frustrate crime. The difference in research approach can be illustrated by interviews with delinquents. This has been a standard method for those trying to understand the influence of family, peers, schools and a host of other factors on the development of delinquent behaviour. Where the purpose is to frustrate crime, however, the interviews concentrate instead on asking delinquents why they committed *particular* crimes and *how* they went about doing this. So the research method may be essentially the same, but the questions are quite different.

But quite often the research methods will also have to change. Focusing on criminals not crime has meant that certain research designs and methodologies have come to dominate criminology. For example, cohort studies and criminal career research have occupied centre stage in the discipline for several decades. To support this research an array of methodologies has been developed which have dominated the journals, including self-reported delinquency measures, psychological assessments, measures of educational attainment and regression analyses. For the new crime prevention agenda much more use would be made of victimization surveys, crime pattern analysis, crime mapping and hot spot analysis. Quite soon, crime mapping will become as much an essential tool of criminological research as statistical analysis is at present.

The broader scholarly ambitions of criminology will also need to be modified. In the typical research project, more weight is given to its internal validity and methodological rigour than to its creativity and insightfulness. Valued least of all is its relevance to solving real-life problems. Consequently, we may come to learn a great deal, for example, about the developmental trajectory of delinquents 20 years ago, but may find this knowledge is of purely historical value. Not only does it come far too late to influence those delinquents' lives, but because so much has changed in society, it might also have little to tell us about dealing with today's delinquency and crime. In fact, in the fast moving world of the future it is likely that criminology will have to sacrifice some scholarly rigour in favour of timeliness and relevance. Techniques of 'rapid appraisal' (Beebe 1995) will need to be employed far more frequently than now, and reports will have to be produced with commensurate speed. If this means that they focus more on results and implications than the details of methodology, so much the better.

CHANGES IN APPLICATION AND AUDIENCE

Focusing more directly on the control of crime will also result in criminologists becoming more interested in intervening upstream rather than downstream in the criminal justice process. Thus they will begin to take more interest in policing than in the later stages of sentencing and treatment. (In fact, correctional treatment has usually been found ineffective, partly because it sees crime as the result of pathology that can be cured rather than of normal human greed and selfishness.) Taking interest in police will not mean, as so often is the case now, adopting a critical stance and studying corruption, brutality and inequitable treatment of minorities. These are important topics, but so is police effectiveness in detecting and arresting offenders. To study this properly, criminologists must accept the essential role played by police in protecting society against crime and must welcome the opportunity to assist with this task.

Business and industry are the main vehicles for bringing new technology into our everyday lives and they are playing an increasingly large role in crime and its control (Felson 1997). Businesses are the victims of huge numbers of unrecorded crimes – for example, employee theft and shoplifting – and for the most part businesses themselves have sought to control these crimes, turning to the security industry, not the police, for assistance they need. Businesses and industry have also had a major role in *creating* crime, through their products and procedures (Hardie and Hobbs 2002). Insecure cars have contributed to the car thefts that comprise large proportions of reported crime in most Western countries, and the mobile phone recently created a wave of thefts and robberies in several European countries (Harrington and Mayhew 2002). Michael Levi (2000) has shown that insecure delivery of credit cards contributed to a large expansion of credit card frauds in the 1990s. These examples of business products and procedures creating crime could be multiplied many times over.

Criminologists of the future will no longer be able to neglect business. They must play their part in evaluating and improving security practice, in designing out crime from products and practices and in helping business protect employees and customers from victimization. This will require a sea change in their attitudes to business, which many criminologists currently view with disdain and suspicion – overlooking the fact that ultimately business and industry make their comfortable lives possible. It will also require criminologists to find ways of undertaking and publishing research without compromising business confidentiality and without harming profits. In future, it is quite possible that business will loom as large in criminology as the criminal justice system does today.

CONCLUSIONS

What if criminologists find the future role outlined above deeply unattractive? After all, most of them entered the discipline with ideals of enlightening society about crime, of helping fashion a humane criminal justice system and of helping reform criminals. They may have invested much of themselves in serving these ideals and few might now be able to see themselves in the technical crime control discussed above. Some might even be fundamentally opposed to it. They may have little wish to co-operate with business, the security industry or even the police. And they may have little interest in developing the expertise needed in telecommunications, transport, retailing, housing, entertainment and the other arenas of everyday life where crime needs to be prevented. They may prefer to continue in what they regard as their primary role of enlightenment and education.

The need for some academic criminologists to fill this role will not disappear. The argument of this paper is not that traditional criminology should be swept away because our knowledge of the roots of criminality will always have to be updated as society changes. Rather, the point being argued is that the criminology needs to pay far more attention than it has done in the past to its practical utility. In any case, there are rather few openings available in universities for those wishing to devote themselves to academic careers. There is much more demand for trained criminologists to assist with crime prevention, security and policing. At present, there is a particular need for appropriately trained crime analysts to assist police in implementing problem-oriented and other forms of intelligence-led policing (Goldstein 2003). Many new crime analysts have degrees not in criminology, but in geography and, sad to say, they may have more to offer police than conventionally educated criminologists.

Training young criminologists to assist crime prevention and security will enable them to take up rewarding careers, making direct use of their criminological knowledge. If departments of criminology do not provide this training, how else will it be provided – because provided it must be? If the past is any guide, new departments will be established specifically to fill this need. Similar forces were behind the mushrooming growth of criminal justice in American universities during the past few decades. These departments were established to undertake operational studies of the criminal justice system (and train those working in the system) – again work disdained by many of those with criminological backgrounds as being 'atheoretical' and mundane. Already one department of crime science has been founded at a major university – the Jill Dando Institute of Crime Science at University College London. The Institute's founders were deeply sceptical that criminology could change and become more focused on reducing crime. This is why they called it an institute of 'crime science' and why they chose to establish it at a university where there was no existing department of criminology to hinder its growth. So in future there could be two separate but related disciplines in the universities – criminology and crime science – serving distinct missions. This could be more realistic in the short term than seeking to change criminology, but it would hold up the supply of the scientifically trained people we need to help in controlling forms of serious crime, such as terrorism and transnational organised crime. Much better would be for more criminologists to transform themselves to meet this urgent need.

ACKNOWLEDGEMENT

Thanks are due to Nick Tilley for helpful comments.

REFERENCES

Beebe, J., Basic concepts and techniques of rapid appraisal. *Human Organization,* 54(1), pp. 42–51 1995.

Clarke, R.V. (Ed.), *Situational Crime Prevention: Successful Case Studies,* 2nd ed. Monsey: Criminal Justice Press, 1997.

Clarke, R.V. and M. Felson (Eds), *Routine Activity and Rational Choice. Advances in Criminological Theory,* Vol. 5. New Brunswick: Transaction Press, 1993.

Felson, M., Technology, business, and crime. In: M. Felson and R.V. Clarke (Eds), *Business and Crime Prevention.* Monsey: Criminal Justice Press, 1997.

Felson, M., *Crime and Everyday Life* (2nd Edition). Thousand Oaks: Pine Forge Press, 1998.

Felson, M. and R.V. Clarke, *Opportunity Makes the Thief: Practical Theory for Crime Prevention.* Police Research Series Paper 98. Policing and Reducing Crime Unit. London: Home Office Research, Development and Statistics Directorate, 1998.

Garland, D., *The Culture of Control: Crime and Social Order in Contemporary Society.* Chicago: University of Chicago Press, 2001.

Goldstein, H., On further developing problem-oriented policing: The most critical need, the major impediments, and a proposal. In: J. Knutsson (Ed.), *Mainstreaming Problem-Oriented Policing. Crime Prevention Studies,* Vol. 15, pp. 13–48, Monsey: Criminal Justice Press, 2003.

Hardie, J. and Hobbs, B., *Partners against Crime. The Role of the Corporate Sector in Tackling Crime.* London: IPPR, 2002.

Harrington, V. and P. Mayhew, *Mobile Phone Theft.* Home Office Research Study, No. 235. London: Home Office, 2002.

Hough, M. and N. Tilley, *Getting the Grease to the Squeak: Research Lessons for Crime Prevention.* Crime Detection and Prevention Series, Paper 85. Police Research Group. London: Home Office, 1998.

Laycock, G., *Launching Crime Science.* London: Jill Dando Institute of Crime Science, University College London, 2003.

Laycock, G., New challenges for law enforcement. *European Journal on Criminal Policy and Research,* 10, pp. 39–53, 2004 (this issue).

Levi, M., *The Prevention of Plastic and Cheque Fraud: A Briefing Paper.* London: Home Office Research, Development and Statistics Directorate, 2000.

Newman, G.R. and R.V. Clarke, *Superhighway Robbery: Preventing E-commerce Crime.* Cullompton: Willan Publishing, 2003.

Pease, K., *Cracking Crime through Design.* London: Design Council, 2001.

Taylor, I., P. Walton and J. Young, *The New Criminology.* London: Routledge & Kegan Paul, 1973.

Von Hirsch, A., D. Garland and A.Wakefield (Eds), *Ethical and Social Issues in Situational Crime Prevention.* Oxford: Hart Publications, 2000.

Wilson, J.Q., *Thinking about Crime.* New York: Basic Books, 1975.

CHAPTER 10

RESEARCH ON CRIME AND TECHNOLOGY

Cindy J. Smith

INTRODUCTION

Technology presents special circumstances for criminologist researchers. To date, much of the crime research has been in areas where the technical aspects of the crime do not interfere with the research. For example, it is not necessary to understand how an automobile is powered to research auto theft. However, new technology has presented new challenges. For example, the researcher must understand how to identify a virus before he or she can count it.

The purpose of this paper is to reflect on the resulting challenges new technology has presented for those who conduct research on the nexus of crime and technology. There are three key issues in this reflection. First, the research development process helps to understand why we do not have more research in the public domain at this time. Next, a discussion of some of the research methods used to date with examples is presented. Finally, this paper presents a discussion of the implications of conducting research in the high-tech sciences along with the responsibilities of the researchers, data owners, and policy-makers.

RESEARCH DEVELOPMENT PROCESS

Cutting edge research follows a general four step developmental process (See Figure 1). Practitioners are often the first to observe a new crime. They discuss it at meetings and write about it in their own newsletters, trade journals, and other publications. Researchers depend on practitioners to raise their awareness to this new concern. For example, practitioners knew about worms (computer viruses) long before the researchers became involved. For example, in this text Ms. Angers from Canada presents:

> There are three ways of committing a crime with a computer; using the computer as a tool (i.e., contact between organized crime figures), using the computer as a storage device (i.e. pornography), and using the computer as a target (i.e., viruses).

The second step occurs when researchers become aware of and interested in the new phenomenon and begin to explore or describe the crime, impact of the event, or simply to count the occurrence while working closely with practitioners. Once the crime, offenders, or victims are sufficiently described, the researchers begin to

Ernesto U. Savona (ed.), Crime and Technology: New Frontiers for Regulations, Law Enforcement and Research, 105–110.

FIGURE 1. Research Development Process

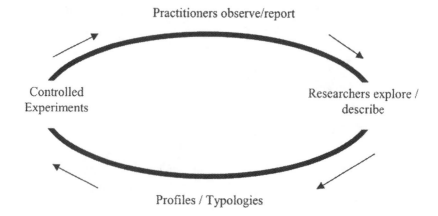

classify or categorize the new crimes. They develop profiles and typologies that are useful in developing controlled experiments or creating theories. The practitioners and researchers discuss these preliminary typologies in terms of the characteristics of the crime as they struggle to generalize and create an abbreviated common language. For example, David Wall described this typology of cybercrime in his text in 2001. There are three categories of cybercrimes:

1. The internet is used as a tool to commit an old crime (i.e., pedophilia, fraud);
2. The internet is used to commit a new crime that did not exist before the technology was developed (i.e., appropriation of music or software); and
3. The internet is used as a communication device (i.e., hate speech, bomb talk).

The research process on technology is currently somewhere between the exploratory step and the profiling step. The good news is that the research development process is progressing comparably to the way other new crimes have progressed through this cycle. Additionally, researchers are beginning to be quite interested, are probably funded at some level and there should be a rapidly growing body of published research over the next few years as the researchers begin to develop controlled experiments, risk and needs assessments, theories and other useful tools.

Throughout the research development process, the researchers and practitioners work simultaneously to raise awareness among the stakeholders. Generally, these stakeholders include raising the awareness of governments of the need for new or revised laws and funding, funding agencies of the need for research, and the general public and/or victims for prevention and intervention.

Within the research literature on high-tech crimes, many articles spend considerable time raising the level of awareness to the seriousness of this or that particular issue by discussing two key points:

1. This problem exists at a much higher rate than currently is known. Evidence for this belief of under reporting is because victims are unaware that they have been

victimized and victims are unwilling to reveal the crime. For example, stock-holders would be upset if they knew a computer system was compromised.

2. This problem is costing a considerable amount of money. Estimates are very high in the literature and include, for example, the loss of current and future sales.

These two key points set the stage for increased funding availability, which results in increased research.

RESEARCH METHODS

What is new in research methods? The answer to that question to date is *not much*. To date the methods used in the research literature have been the same methods used in other research for many years. However, as the research process moves toward con-trolled experiments, it is possible that these methods may need to be expanded, such as those suggested in Dr. Savona's article included in this text. Additionally, there may be a need to expand the analytical techniques, such as those suggested by Hans DeRoo, also found in this text. However, for now, the old methods appear to be sufficient during this exploratory research era.

A survey of the literature to date includes a wide variety of methods. For example, one study (Dertouzos et al., 1999) used secondary data. In this study the researchers sufficiently gained the confidence and trust of the data owners and were able to obtain and analyze the data. Gaining trust is a key issue when researching sensitive materials. For example, the Dertouzos (1999) study determined the economic costs of high-tech hardware theft using manufacturing and security costs from computer firms.

Next, the Delphi method was used to predict future types of computer crimes (Coutorie, 1995). This widely used method compared the predictions of high-tech criminal justice experts with the predictions of techies to determine what types of crimes would become more prevalent in future years.

The third method is observation. One study observed the behaviour of those par-ticipating in a newsgroup – alt.drugs.chemistry – that educated participants on how to make synthetic drugs (Schneider, 2003). The second study observed that internet users who were going to a legitimate website were found to be quite likely to try to download illegal material once at the site (Demetriou & Silke, 2003).

Additionally, survey and case study methods also appear in the literature (Dertouzos et al., 1999). A comparative study authored jointly by researchers from US and India developed a model that tests the economic benefits of maintaining dif-ferent or incompatible DVD standards across geographic regions to prevent piracy (Chellappa & Shivendu, 2003). Finally, interviews were conducted with 13 convicted men who downloaded child porn (Quayle & Taylor, 2002).

CHALLENGES OF HIGH-TECH CRIME

The challenges that high-tech crimes pose to researchers are not very different than other new crimes or new methods of crime have posed to researchers in the past. The first challenge is the ability to access the data. There are four possible explanations for this challenge: 1) unfamiliarity of the way crimes are committed or newness of some of the crimes; 2) new vocabulary, as discussed in the Hans De Roo article in this text; 3) difficulty in understanding the technology; and 4) lack of partnerships, which is discussed later in this article.

The second challenge is accurately and completely interpreting the findings. This is as a result of the technical language and nuances of the technology. For example, when Demetriou & Silke (2003) designed their sting operation to tempt internet users to download illegal material, they logged his website with various search engines with words indicating the legal activities found on the website. His intention was to attract non-deviant individuals and see if they would commit an illegal activity once they were on the website. However, some search engines conduct word searches, which enabled some visitors to come to the website expecting to find the illegal material. While this is a very basic piece of search engine information, those not adequately schooled in technology or not partnering with a techie would have included the "intentional deviants" in the findings with the non-deviants.

Three policy implications related to these challenges are found; 1) count crime, 2) develop partnerships, and 3) learn technology basics. First, baseline databases must be developed. In other words, there exists a need to count things. For years Freda Adler, who is well known to ISPAC members, has promoted simply counting things. The first step in researching crime is to understand how much of it exists – in other words, count it. Graeme Newman (2003), in the Expert meeting on the World Crime and Justice Report 2004-2005, highlighted the importance of counting by suggesting we count all true threats to human security, such as homicide rates. In fact, he suggests that we increase the number of items that we routinely count to develop a social vulnerability index. Counting is not an easy task. This takes considerable trust that the data will be used appropriately and that the member states or corporations will be held harmless.

It is not likely that researchers will become experts in all areas necessary to conduct good research. For example, researchers will not become experts in technology, experts in research, and experts in crime, plus learn the necessary diplomatic behaviour to obtain the data. Therefore, it would be wise to develop partnerships (See Figure 2). These partnerships must include the data owner – the corporation, the victim, or the government. It must include a techie, who can assist in the design, collection, and interpretation of the data to ensure high quality data and that the fine distinctions are included. Lastly, a researcher must be included in the partnership to ensure that the data collected are the type of data that will be useful for research that will inform policy.

Finally, the researchers must learn technology basics to ensure accurate and complete communication between the partners. The researchers who do policy relevant research often partner with practitioners who know considerably more about the topic or data than the researcher. An appropriate level of respect, humility, and effort to learn the basics will increase the effectiveness of the partnership.

FIGURE 2

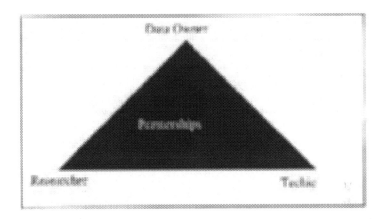

RESPONSIBILITIES OF RESEARCHERS AND POLICY-MAKERS

Researchers and policy-makers have several separate responsibilities. It is the responsibility of the researcher to be trustworthy, confidential, and use the scientific method. In this text, Lucy Angers suggests that researchers should be more responsible, ensuring the data reported are accurate, complete, and interpreted in the context in which they exist. Researchers must build trust by being trustworthy in their behaviour. Additionally, researchers have a responsibility to hold appropriate information in confidence when gaining access to sensitive information. This includes aggregating data in such a way that the victims, perpetrator, and country or corporation are not identifiable – especially if it is embarrassing to anyone involved and to ensure false accusations are not perpetuated. Finally, researchers have a responsibility to conduct quality scientific research. This includes random assignment where appropriate, using control groups, discussing limitations and educating all members of the partnership about why a particular method is best. Additionally, the partnership must use language that is understandable and useful to policy-makers and the readership.

Data owners and policy-makers have responsibilities also. It is imperative that the data owners provide a structure and climate of willingness to participate in research to enable researchers to count and later conduct controlled experiments, risk and needs assessments, or other research to help guide policy. By providing the opportunity, structure, and climate to partner in research efforts, the data owners ensure that policy is based on the state-of-the-art knowledge. Policy makers have a responsibility to use quality reliable research results to inform policy.

REFERENCES

Chellappa, R. and S. Shivendu, Economic implications of variable technology standards for movie piracy in a global context. *Journal of Management Information Systems,* 20(2), pp. 137–168, 2003.

Coutorie, L., The future of high-technology crime: A parallel Delphi study. *Journal of criminal justice,* 23 (1), pp. 13, 1995.

Demetriou, C. and A. Silke, A criminological internet 'sting.' *British Journal of Criminology,* 43, pp. 213–222, 2003.

Dertouzos, J., E. Larson, and P. Ebener, *The economic costs and implications of high-technology hardware theft.* Santa Monica, CA: Rand, 1999.

Quayle, E. and M. Taylor, Child pornography and the internet: Perpetuating a cycle of abuse. *Deviant Behavior: An Interdisciplinary Journal,* 23, pp. 331–361, 2002.

Newman, G., World crime trends: Notes on recommendations for the second global report on crime and justice. *Expert Meeting on the World Crime and Justice Report, 2004–2005,* Turin, Italy, June 2003.

Schneider. J., Hiding in plain sight: An exploration of the illegal (?) activities of a drugs news-group. *Howard Journal,* 42(4), pp. 374, 2003.

Wall, D.S., CyberCrimes and the Internet. In Wall, D.S. (ed), *Crime and the Internet,* pp.1–17. London: Routledge, 2001.

CHAPTER 11

CRIME MAPPING AND THE TRAINING NEEDS OF LAW ENFORCEMENT

Jerry H. Ratcliffe

INTRODUCTION

Since the mid-1980s, reductions in the cost of computing power and digital data storage have combined with a rationalisation of computer operating systems to enable the wide dissemination of a range of new technologies for crime fighting. With the computerisation of police records for statistical and managerial purposes came a realisation that these same records could be employed for crime and intelligence analysis, and in some cases crime mapping. Law enforcement interest in using geographical information systems (GIS) to map the incidence of crime occurred in parallel to research activities that identified patterns in crimes and criminal behaviour in the emerging field of environmental criminology (see, among others, Brantingham and Brantingham 1981; Bottoms and Wiles 1992; Rengert 1992; Bottoms and Wiles 2002). This development of practitioner interest in crime mapping alongside a research field dedicated to understanding the importance of place in offender behaviour and victimisation could be said to mimic and draw from a similar two-pronged thrust within geography. At the time, geographers were developing both GIS and geographical information science.

This paper outlines the development of spatial systems and thinking, before proceeding to summarise activities in three areas of mapping that have become influential within law enforcement: hotspot mapping for crime analysis, CompStat mapping, and geographic profiling. The paper concludes by using a simple model of intelligence-led crime reduction to consider future training needs within the law enforcement arena, so that maximum benefit is derived from mapping technologies.

SPATIAL SYSTEMS AND SPATIAL SCIENCE

Spatial analysis has for the last two decades or so been moving forward on two fronts; statistical spatial analysis and spatial modelling (Fischer et al. 1996). First there has

This chapter was previously published in *European Journal on Criminal Policy and Research* **10**: 65–83, 2004.

Ernesto U. Savona (ed.), Crime and Technology: New Frontiers for Regulations, Law Enforcement and Research, 111–128.
© 2004 *Springer. Printed in The Netherlands.*

been an increase in the development of statistical spatial tools, culminating in the recent development of geographically weighted regression techniques (Fotheringham et al. 2002). Secondly, and arguably more usefully for crime reduction planning and policy, there has been an expansion in the number of techniques available for exploratory spatial data analysis (ESDA), techniques that can be applied in a spatial modelling environment to reveal crime patterns and hotspots.

ESDA is an extension of exploratory data analysis (EDA), which is commonly used in a number of research fields. ESDA expands on EDA by explicitly examining and considering the spatial component of the data. Although most crime data could be considered to have a spatial aspect, ESDA explores patterns in the data from a pre-dominantly geographic angle, such that other relationships between datum points are either of secondary consideration or are used to compliment and refine the spatial analysis. This is not to negate the value of other data variables within crime records: Other non-spatial features within crime records have been found to provide valuable insight into offender behaviour, especially temporal (Ratcliffe 2002) and modus operandi (Bennell and Canter 2002; Yokota and Watanabe 2002) variables. Within the data analysis phase of a study, ESDA promotes the spatial exploration to the forefront of the analysis, and with this increased interest have come a range of new and inno-vative spatial processes designed to uncover geographical patterns within data.

The development of many ESDA techniques from academic research interest into mainstream computer applications has enabled a cohort of criminal justice practi-tioners to uncover the patterns in their own data and drive new ways to view the crim-inal justice system, and in particular the law enforcement environment. This facet of geographical science can not be overstated enough – spatial analysis techniques are changing the way that many in criminal justice are doing business. Examples that will be discussed in this paper include geographic profiling for serial crime investigations and middle management accountability processes for law enforcement, commonly known as CompStat meetings.

While one cohort of practitioners has embraced the new GIS technology and are starting to uncover the possibilities that emerge from the use of GIS, others have still to be exposed to the value of a spatial understanding of crime patterns. Some are reluctant to embrace the use of GIS within the organisational framework of the work-place, preferring to leave GIS outside the central sanctum of decision-making and policy formulation. Within many areas of policing, there is still in a failure to inte-grate spatial thinking into the core decision-making process at either a tactical or strategic level, even though GIS are currently being applied in many countries at a range of spatial and organisational levels. It has been argued by Stan Openshaw, a pioneer of spatial analysis, that although there are risks when a GIS is employed poorly to a policy situation, there is an equivalent 'crime' of not using GIS when it would enhance the policy decision (Openshaw 1993). For example purposes, the next sections will provide an overview of some key applications of GIS within the lawen-forcement environment. The paper then continues to discuss the future training needs of organisations so that an objective spatial understanding of crime can become more central to decision-making.

CRIME MAPPING

For at least the last 100 years police officers have stuck pins into paper maps displayed on walls, where each pin represented a crime location. In some places this practice continues. Although a pin in a map is certainly a 'crime map', this paper does not seek to refer to this technologically unsophisticated method of mapping crime as 'crime mapping', but reserves the term, and the following discussion, for the modern conjunction of two disciplines, crime research and geographical information science. The geographical community have for some time now utilised the abbreviation GIS for both geographical information systems and geographical information science (which is sometimes abbreviated as GISc). The distinction is relevant for this paper, as the former refers to a tool consisting of hardware, software, data, people and organizations for the collecting, storing, analysing and disseminating of information relating to the earth (Chrisman 2002: 12). For many practitioners this is realised in the form of a software package that sits on a desktop computer. The second description of GIS as a 'science' embodies the concept of a developing set of analytical processes, techniques and methods which advance spatial understanding. The development of crime mapping has required advances in both systems and the science.

In the early development of crime mapping, translating the systems from the specialist research area of geography to the practitioner environment of criminal justice practice caused some difficulties. The police were the first criminal justice agency to take a real interest in GIS, and remain the main supporters of crime mapping to this day. Early attempts at implementation were beset by technical issues and the incompatibility of police databases (Hirschfield et al. 1995), geocoding (the method by which a street address is converted into map coordinates) problems (Craglia et al. 2000) and management difficulties (Openshaw et al. 1990).

However once the early innovators had ironed out many of these technical difficulties, it was possible to expand the range of agencies that used computer mapping packages to map the instance of crime (Weisburd 2001). Much of this innovation was driven in the US by the Crime Mapping Research Center (CMRC), established in 1997 by the National Institute of Justice. Although a US agency, the influence of the CMRC extended beyond the continent and had a significant impact on the development of crime mapping systems in the UK, Australia and Europe. Now renamed the Mapping and Analysis for Public Safety program (www.ojp.usdoj.gov/nij/maps/), the NIJ program continues to provide free support and some software to law enforcement agencies experimenting with crime mapping, as well as provide grants that are strategically targeted to advance the field.

Crime mapping has therefore grown to be a significant player in the practitioner market: searching the National Criminal Justice Reference Service (www.ncjrs.org) for 'crime mapping' elicits over 100 hits, and on the popular search engine Google (www.google.com) the same search found over a quarter of a million hits (as of January 2004). For a recent history of crime mapping in the US, see LaVigne and Groff (2001), while a longer history of the field can be found in Weisburd and McEwen (1997).

FIGURE 1. A basic 'pin' map of recorded vehicle crime locations in Philadelphia, Pennsylvania (USA) for July 2002. In the map, each crime location is represented by a small black dot. For US readers familiar with the city, the major interstate roads are indicated and labelled.

Hotspot Mapping

Figure 1 shows an example of a rudimentary crime map, depicting vehicle crime locations in the US city of Philadelphia for July 2002. Automated pin mapping, such as can be found in Figure 1, provide a basic mechanism to convert a recorded crime database into spatial features (Harries 1999). The limitations of this rudimentary mechanism are well documented (Harries 1999; Ratcliffe 2001) and include problems of points that overlap, human inability to determine clusters, and the difficulty in establishing broad trends in point data. The problem of information overload and not being able to "see the wood for the trees" is evident in Figure 1. From a managerial perspective however, automated crime maps (like Figure 1) that could be easily updated and mapped using customisable search algorithms tailored to the specific

FIGURE 2. Same data source as Figure 1, except this time the points have been replaced by a kernel density surface which emphasises the crime hotspot locations at the expense of being able to determine individual crime locations. Although this could be considered a less accurate map, the image is still useful for police operational purposes and is also suitable for sharing with the public as it avoids identifying individual crime victims.

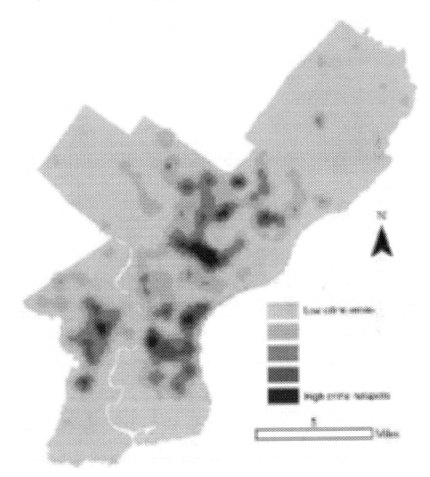

request of the user, advanced crime analysis significantly (Rich 1995). While the systems component of GIS has been advancing from a user perspective, the 'science' component has been advancing from the research direction.

The limitations of crime mapping and the difficulties with data overload as can be seen in Figure 1 have been overcome in recent years with exploratory data techniques such as kernel density smoothing (Gatrell and Dunn 1995; McLafferty et al. 2000) and cluster analysis (Ekblom 1988; Nelson et al. 2001). The same data for Figure 1 can be viewed using a kernel density surface that refines the display to emphasise the crime hotspots (Figure 2). From a law enforcement management perspective, this has significant value. Operational policing can be enhanced by concentrating activity on crime hotspots, one of the areas where police can have a significant impact on crime (Weisburd et al. 1993; Weisburd and Green 1995; Sherman et al. 1998).

The improvements in GIS over the last 20 years have resulted in a situation where the desktop market is dominated by two commercial companies, MapInfo and ESRI (the most commonly used tools being the MapInfo suite of programs and Arc View and Arc GIS by ESRI). Although this does not negate the use of remote sensing applications and other programs for specialized law enforcement use (for example drug enforcement officers at national borders may monitor satellite imagery), the primary use of GIS in the policing domain is in the area of property and violent crime mapping. While the market dominance of MapInfo and ESRI provides little advantage to users in terms of competition and pricing, the contraction of the field to two dominant systems had meant that developers seeking to advance the field of crime mapping have only to consider compatibility issues with two types of GIS structure. This rationalisation of the 'system' area of GIS has therefore enabled smaller developers and researchers to concentrate on advancing the 'science' aspect of GIS. As a result, advanced crime mappers in police departments across the world are able to map crime, disorder and calls for service, compare crime distributions to the underlying features of unemployment, race and other socio-economic data, and generate hotspot maps for intelligence use. As an example, Figure 2 shows the same data as Figure 1, except that the data has been run through a hotspot algorithm using a software program called HotSpot Detective^{TM}. This program applies a particular range of spatial and temporal algorithms to crime data, but a more complete review of spatio-temporal crime analysis routines, with an application, can be found in Ratcliffe (2004a). In Figure 2, the computer program generates a hotspot surface map showing the hotspots of crime without having the distraction of hundreds of individual points.

Hotspots have taken on a significant prominence in policing in a number of countries. For example, the evaluation of a range of crime prevention measures by Sherman and co-workers found that concentrated hotspot policing was one of the few policing activities that could demonstrate measurable long-term crime prevention and reduction (Sherman et al. 1998). In the UK, hotspot crime and disorder problems are one of the four tactical problems that are deemed important enough to tackle within the framework of the National Intelligence Model (NCIS 2000; Flood 2004). Hotspot mapping technologies have advanced rapidly and are now one of the central features of CrimeStat, a publicly available and free software package supported by the US National Institute of Justice.

Mapping technologies similar to this have been used within the criminal justice system to map a wide variety of crime-related phenomena, including temporal patterns of high volume crime in Sydney, Australia (Ratcliffe 2002) and city crime patterns for operational management and CompStat purposes (McGuire 2000). Indeed CompStat, in its many forms, has been one of the main driving forces in advancing law enforcement use of crime mapping and is discussed in the following section.

CompStat

CompStat (abbreviated from Computer Statistics) rose to prominence in the New York City Police Department (NYPD) in the early 1990s, where precinct captains were presented with maps of crime distribution at regular meetings, and were required to respond to local crime patterns and reduce the crime level. CompStat has been described as a "goal-oriented strategic management process that uses computer technology, operational strategy, and managerial accountability to structure the manner in which a police department provides crime-control services" (Walsh 2001: 347). CompStat is not a crime mapping method *per se*, but it is a significant application area for crime mapping techniques and conference presentations often discuss the best way to integrate crime mapping into the CompStat meeting format. Although the whole CompStat process is one of managerial accountability, crime mapping became the central pillar and medium through which a room full of senior police officers could observe the effectiveness (or not!) of a police commander. Now widely adopted throughout the USA and beyond, CompStat has been described as a paradigm shift in operational policing. This is probably the case, introduced as it was into a police culture that was (and still is in the majority of places) fixated with internal rules, managerial procedures and local efficiency rather than any external indication of police effectiveness (Goldstein 1990).

The CompStat model has travelled far and wide. At the 2003 meeting of the International Association of Chiefs of Police (IACP), the Philadelphia Police Department (USA) shared a platform with the Thames Valley Police (UK) in a session that explored how the Philadelphia model had been translated to the British context. Furthermore, the New SouthWales Police Service (Australia) equivalent has been thoroughly evaluated for its crime reduction effect. Termed an Operations and Crime Review (OCR), the New South Wales model works in a similar vein to that in New York City. In a large meeting room with up to 100 police officers, a number of different local area commands are brought to the fore and presented with the patterns of crime since their last attendance at an OCR, a period of about three months. The local area commander is then required to explain what major crime patterns have occurred since his or her last attendance, and the activity that police are currently undertaking. Most importantly, the local area commander is required to explain what they will do over the next three months to combat the crime problems that are displayed on three large screens in the room. Notes are taken for review at the commencement of the next meeting attended by representatives of that local area command. The strength of the process lies in the rapid conversion of crime data into map-ready form enabling a large audience to quickly determine the location of crime hotspots.

Problems with CompStat lie less with the mapping component than with the organisational element. CompStat requires flexible leadership from operational commanders, a knowledge of 'what works' and 'what is promising' in policing tactics, as well as the bravery to experiment with different crime reduction strategies in a live operational context. As Walsh is right to point out, "this process of operational experimentation is challenging the core beliefs and attitudes of many police managers about what constitutes effective policing" (Walsh 2001: 348). The main problem with CompStat is that it challenges police managers in areas in which they have never been required to be effective. Few police commanders have ever been trained in crime reduction or how to interpret criminal intelligence analysis products such as crime maps. This situation is analogous to teaching a group of students mathematics and then setting a test on English literature. In other words, the criteria used to determine suitability for promotion within contemporary law enforcement rarely include knowledge and ability to effect long term crime reduction, yet this is exactly the skill that CompStat demands. Only recently have crime reduction measures been used as a performance indicator, and the rest of the policing management system has yet to catch up to this new paradigm.

Geographic Profiling

While CompStat is an operational management process, geographic profiling is an investigative methodology. Geographic profiling is an investigative technique designed to aid police investigations into serial crimes. In essence it aims to provide a spatial profile of a possible offender in rather the same manner as a psychological profile. While a psychological report can provide some clues as to the mental state and demographic characteristics of an offender, a geographic profile can suggest areas where the offender might live or work. The field of geographic profiling has grown from the innovative combination of a number of spatial theoretical concepts, the most significant being environmental criminology (Brantingham and Brantingham 1981). The Brantinghams' crime pattern theory provides a framework for offender search patterns in their hunt for crime opportunities, and is itself derived from a combination of routine activity theory (Cohen and Felson 1979; Brantingham and Brantingham 1993) and opportunity theory (Jeffery and Zahm 1993), also known as the rational choice perspective (Cornish and Clarke 1986; Clarke and Felson 1993; Newman 1997).

These theories state that most people will develop a routine activity to their lives such that they will go from home to work at around a certain time, travel from work to recreation activities, and then from the recreational activities to home. This is of course hugely simplistic, but the broader concept is that people develop certain places that they commonly frequent (such as home, work, school, restaurants, bars, movie theatres and so on). These *nodes* become comfortable places which feel secure and where people spend a considerable amount of time. The *paths* that run from node to node are also areas where people feel comfortable and relatively secure, due to the feeling of being in familiar circumstances. The Brantinghams' argue that offenders will have similar routine activities in their lives, but these areas of familiarity will also be the search areas for opportunities to offend. While Cohen and Felson's Routine Activity Theory can be interpreted as an indication of victim behaviour (Robinson 1999), crime pattern theory can be considered the offender equivalent (Brantingham and Brantingham 1993), indicating areas of likely criminal behaviour. At the coming together of the victim and the offender is a rational choice by the offender to take advantage (or not) of any criminal opportunity that is presented (Cornish and Clarke 1986; Clarke and Felson 1993).

Geographic profiling pulls these ideas together to deconstruct a pattern of offending elicited from victim information and crime scene examination resulting in a map of crime sites such that each point represents a location where the offender was known to be, at one point in time. Knowledge of journey-to-crime research assists in the interpretation. Journey-to-crime research builds on the least effort principle which states that most people will not travel further than necessary to achieve a goal. For example, few people will travel from one town to another in order to buy bread as this common commodity can usually be purchased close to home. Offenders similarly rarely travel further than necessary to commit crime, as increased distance requires additional effort and increases risk. Offenders therefore search closer to home for criminal opportunities, and usually within their routine activity or *awareness* space.

From the crime site clues and with extensive knowledge of general offender behaviour, a process known as aggregate criminal spatial behaviour (Brantingham and Brantingham 1984), geographic profiling can estimate the likelihood that a key *node* for the offender is in a certain area. The eventual output from the computerised spatial analysis routine is a surface map of risk which identifies the likelihood of residence of the offender by area. Areas that have a higher likelihood of offender residence are more likely to have either a home or workplace of the offender in those areas.

The application possibilities for geographic profiling are substantial. Given that a rudimentary geographic profile can be constructed for a crime pattern based on as little as six offence sites (Rossmo 1995a), the process can be used on a number of different crime types. Geographic profiling can be used for suspect prioritisation, patrol saturation, enhancements to police information systems, linking with an outside agency database, and most recently to target DNA testing of large populations. The process has been mainly used for serial homicide and arson investigations (Canter and Larkin 1993; Rossmo 1995b; Rossmo 1997; Canter et al. 2000; Rossmo 2000) but the processes of journey-to-crime research and geographic profiling have also been applied to residential burglary studies (Barker 2000; Wiles and Costello 2000), and could theoretically be used for most crime types that have an outdoor opportunity structure (such as vehicle theft and robbery). Geographic profiles have been provided by investigators trained by Environmental Criminology Research Inc (www.ecricanada.com) on a variety of high profile cases, including the Washington sniper investigation, where Professor Kim Rossmo was invited to provide a geographic profile as an investigative aid.

While the techniques of geographic profiling are still being refined, and some studies suggest that the technique has limitations for some offender types (Santtila et al. 2003), the research aspect of this field is growing, providing newcases to act as test beds for technique adaptation. Rossmo claims a high success rate for geographic profiling (Rossmo 2000) and ongoing work by the UK Home Office is currently exploring the socio-economic applications of the geographic profiling methodology as a possible apparatus to establish a more strategic understanding of offender behaviour in space.

MOVING FORWARD WITH GIS

The range of spatial analytical options that have opened up for crime analysts over recent years clearly has training implications for the criminal justice system. Police crime analysts in particular are often under pressure to be not only familiar with the latest techniques but also how to apply those techniques in an practical crime analysis situation. As with any developing field, the route to an established analytical regime is paved with many dead ends or techniques that are only in vogue for a few years and are quickly superseded by superior methods. One example is STAC, a program for the spatial and temporal analysis of crime (ICJIA 1996). Although popular in the United States for a number of years as a hotspot surface mapping tool, the methodology has been found to be arbitrary and unsuitable by a number of researchers (Bowers and Hirschfield 1999; Ratcliffe and McCullagh 1999; Craglia et al. 2000). The real strength of STAC was to provide a starting point for the development of more powerful techniques, and to establish the need for such tools within the research and practitioner community. In this latter role, STAC established itself as a pioneering technique within the field of spatial crime analysis.

It would be natural, given the rapid development of spatial crime analysis as a field, that the major cause of concern would be the establishment of training regimes for crime analysts. After all, the plethora of appropriate techniques that add value to crime information (some of which are described earlier in this paper) would suggest that the training of analysts is a fundamental issue, and in many cases this is true. However there is another, more pressing training concern that becomes apparent when we use a simple model of intelligence-led crime reduction to explore the broader picture of crime control.

This model of crime control, from Ratcliffe (2003), is shown in Figure 3. In this model, the role of the intelligence unit (the usual home of the police crime analyst) is to interpret the criminal environment. It is in this role that spatial crime analysis techniques are applied to crime data in order to ascertain a picture of the crime situation. The importance of this analytical role can not be underestimated within the framework of intelligence-led policing. For example, the UK National Intelligence Model focuses on only four analytical situations, one of which is the identification of crime and disorder hotspots of which crime mapping is an essential technique (NCIS 2000). However the identification of crime hotspots is not the end of the story. As can be seen in Figure 3, this new intelligence has to be communicated to a decision-maker, someone who is either within the police service or in a relevant crime prevention arena. The intelligence gathered from the analysis (spatial and aspatial) must be used to influence the thinking of the decision-maker. Without the ability to communicate intelligence to decision-makers, analysts will find that their role achieves little and has no impact on the criminal environment.

The final stage of the model (Figure 3) requires the decision-maker to use the intelligence provided by the analyst to influence their choice of crime reduction and prevention strategy so that an effective crime reduction regime can be implemented. Only if this final stage of 'impact' occurs will the intelligence-led crime reduction process be complete. The overall model places equal significance on the ability of the intelligence analyst to interpret the criminal environment as it does the need for the decision-maker to influence it. With this model there are therefore three areas of training attention. One places a responsibility on the analyst, in that the analyst has to be able to interpret the criminal environment. The influence arm of the model places equal weight on the analyst and the decision-maker, in that the former has to explain the criminal intelligence and the latter has to understand the intelligence. The final arm of the model places the responsibility squarely on the shoulders of decision-makers.

Where Are the Training Needs?

From this observer's perspective, itwould seem that the crime analysis field is making more progress in training and education of crime analysts than general policing has made in the police leadership arena. At the time of writing, the International Association of Crime Analysts are finalising a certification programme, complete with a training handbook and pre-packaged classes, which has a complete area dedicated to spatial analysis techniques (details of the new training programme can be found at www.iaca.net). Similarly, the International Association of Law Enforcement Intelligence Analysts (IALEIA) advertises dedicated crime mapping training sessions through its web site (www.ialeia.org).

A number of police services throughout the world also offer their officers dedicated mapping training. For example, the New South Wales Police Service, Australia's largest, has offered dedicated crime mapping training to all of its crime analysts for many years, and the New Zealand Police have mapping training for their Intranet mapping service, the Map-based Analytical Policing System (NZP 2002). The New York City Police Department use mapping as the information basis for their CompStat process (McGuire 2000), and this is mimicked in the New South Wales Police Service equivalent, the OCR (Chilvers and Weatherburn 2001). The Metropolitan Police (UK), one of Europe's largest police services, has also had an analyst training programme that sets aside significant portions of the programme to spatial analysis. The desire to professionalize and provide analytical utility is therefore driving the law enforcement crime analysis field to train itself in spatial crime analysis.

The second stage of the model in Figure 3 is to use crime analysis intelligence to influence decision-makers. Within a law enforcement environment it is usual that the initial decision-maker is a local commander. It is at this point that questions arise as to the state of the police leadership field in regard to understanding intelligence and acting on crime analysis information. As an indication, consider the training catalogue of the International Association of Chiefs of Police (IACP). The 2004 catalogue

FIGURE 3. *A model of intelligence-led crime reduction.* Source: *Ratcliffe, 2003.*

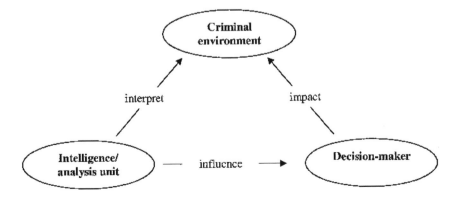

TABLE 1. Main categories of programs offered in the 2004 IACP training catalogue.

Program category	Number of courses offered
Quality leadership	5
Community involvement	8
Management and supervision	12
Crisis management	3
Force management and integrity issues	8
Staffing, personnel and legal issues	9
Patrol operations and tactical responses	13
Investigations	10

lists all of the programs offered across the US (www.iacp.org/training/ 2004IACPTrainingCatalog.pdf). The IACP offered 68 different programs throughout 2004 in the US, organised into categories. The main categories of program are itemised in Table 1.

None of the 'Quality Leadership' line of programs offer courses on crime prevention or reduction and none of the leadership programs address crime reduction or prevention as sub themes. Only one of the 68 programs explicitly addresses problem-oriented policing, intelligence-led policing or general crime prevention and reduction. The Initiating Preventive Policing program is a 2-day course offered twice in 2004. There are a small number of programs that also address crime reduction, though only in specific situations;[1] Reducing School Violence (a two-day program offered three times); Civil Remedies for Nuisance Abatement (a two-day program offered once); and, Preventing and Reducing Elderly Victimization (a two-day program offered twice throughout the year). There are two courses that are pitched at crime analysts: a three-day introduction course (offered twice) and a single three-day advanced class.

Therefore in summary, the training regime offered to police in the US by the leading police chiefs organisation only has one of 68 programs dedicated to general crime prevention, and only three courses that address crime reduction in specific situations. These programs total 16 days of training offered. By comparison, the number of training days dedicated to SWAT tactics and management is 48.

This is not intended as a direct criticism of the IACP. On the contrary – they provide a wide range of programs that are essential to the general management of a local police service as well as a suite of courses that address specific needs. They rely on feedback from their clients as to the training needs of the law enforcement population. It does however indicate that from the training programme there is a sense that police leadership

---

1   The Enhancing Community Policing with the Media class mentions crime reduction but only in connection with the management of the media.

(in the US at least) does not perceive that it should be aware of the new processes within crime analysis, nor of how to apply criminal intelligence and crime analysis to crime reduction or problem solving. There is no specific training in long-term crime reduction philosophies such as intelligence-led policing or problem-oriented policing.

This is not to say that problem-oriented policing or intelligence-led policing are not popular and supported. In the UK, there is, among some commentators, a desire to see the National Intelligence Model integrate the dominant policing strategy – intelligence-led policing – with the more globally recognised problem-oriented policing (Tilley 2003), and in the US, Scott remains cautiously optimistic in regard to the future of problem-oriented policing, twenty years after its inception (Scott 2000). Although disconcerting to some observers (Whyte 2003) GIS is playing a central role in the Crime and Disorder Audits that have become mandatory in the UK as a result of the Crime and Disorder Act 1998.

Both intelligence-led policing and problem-oriented policing demand high quality information and intelligence analysis so that tactics can be accurately targeted to the right place in a timely manner. In this demand for quality analysis, they do not differ. This broadband recognition that quality crime analysis is the bedrock of any modern crime reduction strategy is driving the crime analysis field to respond and the future seems bright for the quality of crime analysis. The difficulty stems from the lag in training managers to understand and apply the intelligence and analysis that they are presented with.

Training for police managers is a complicated process because they rarely have much free time, and the available space within their training regimes for crime reduction is even more limited. There appears to be an implicit assumption that as senior officers have risen through the ranks of the police service, they have absorbed all they need to know about crime reduction. It would appear that there is a notion that just by being in the police for some time they must know how to 'do' crime reduction. The corollary of this is that there is therefore no real perceived need to teach crime reduction or prevention, as evidenced by Table I. This would appear to be a mistake, as there is evidence that intelligence analysis is still required to 'convince' management of its value (McDowell 1998; Gill 2000; HMIC 2001; Ratcliffe 2004b). This is not to negate the value of training managers in business planning, budgets and personnel issues. However, crime prevention remains the core business of the police and this has not changed since 1829 (Mayne 1829).

CONCLUSION

The broader area of crime mapping would appear to either be, or on the verge of becoming, a fundamental tool in the criminal justice system and in law enforcement in particular. Specific methodologies such as spatio-temporal mapping and geographic profiling provide practitioners with analytical tools that were not previously available without considerable effort. Practitioners (and a few academics) in the fields of crime analysis and intelligence have been quick to realise the training requirements and have been gearing their respective organisations to provide the necessary instruction so that the analytical benefit of the new spatial technologies can be realised. However, the much wider field of police leadership and management has yet to fully embrace the changes that have been happening within the field of crime analysis, leaving a knowledge gap between crime analysts and law enforcement managers. However advanced crime analysis becomes, unless it has the capacity to influence decision-making and thinking at the levels that can actually drive positive change in the criminal environment and the crime level, then all the advances in geographic information systems and science will show little investment return.

While crime analysis still has a long way to go, it is moving ahead at a quick rate and growing in significance. However the opportunities presented by techniques that have been available for some time do not yet appear to be on the radar of police managers. GIS is yet to be fully established as a central player in the criminal justice system but the long term future would appear to be fairly positive if the current paradigms of intelligenceled policing and problem-oriented policing remain at the forefront of police thinking. If police management training can embrace the benefits of these new ideas, from a crime analyst's perspective, there may indeed be a light at the end of the tunnel, and for once it might not be a train coming the other way. The challenge for the immediate future of crime reduction is less to worry about the training of analysts and more to address the inability of law enforcement management to understand and act on the crime analysis they are given.

REFERENCES

Barker, M., The criminal range of small town burglars. In: D. Canter and L. Alison (Eds), *Profiling Property Crimes,* pp. 59–73. London: Ashgate, 2000.

Bennell, C. and D. Canter, Linking commercial burglaries by modus operandi: Tests using regression and ROC analysis. *Science and Justice*, 42(3), pp. 153–164, 2002.

Bottoms, A.E. and P. Wiles, Explanations of crime and place. In: D.J. Evans, N.R. Fyfe and D.T. Herbert (Eds), *Crime, Policing and Place: Essays in Environmental Criminology*, pp. 11–35. London: Routledge, 1992.

Bottoms, A.E. and P. Wiles, Environmental criminology. In: M. Maguire, R. Morgan and R. Reiner (Eds), *The Oxford Handbook of Criminology*, pp. 620–656. London: Oxford University Press, 2002.

Bowers, K.J. and A. Hirschfield, Exploring the link between crime and disadvantage in northwest England: An analysis using geographical information systems. *International Journal of Geographical Information Science*, 13(2), pp. 159–184, 1999.

Brantingham, P.J. and P.L. Brantingham, *Environmental Criminology*. Prospect Heights: Waveland Press, 1981.

Brantingham, P.J. and P.L. Brantingham, *Patterns in Crime*. New York: Macmillan, 1984.

Brantingham, P.L. and P.J. Brantingham, Environment, routine, and situation: Toward a pattern theory of crime. In: R.V. Clarke and M. Felson (Eds), *Routine Activity and Rational Choice*, pp. 259–294. New Brunswick: Transaction Publishers, 1993.

Canter, D., T. Coffey, M. Huntley and C. Missen, Predicting serial killers' home base using a decision support system. *Quantitative Criminology,* 16(4), pp. 457–478, 2000.

Canter, D. and P. Larkin, The environmental range of serial rapists. *Environmental Psychology*, 13(1), pp. 63–69, 1993.

Chilvers, M. and D. Weatherburn, Do targeted arrests reduce crime? *Contemporary Issues in Crime and Justice (NSW Bureau of Crime Statistics and Research)*, 63, pp. 1–16, 2001.

Chrisman, N., *Exploring Geographic Information Systems*. New York: Wiley, 2002.

Clarke, R.V. and M. Felson, Introduction: Criminology, routine activity, and rational choice. In: R.V. Clarke and M. Felson (Eds), *Routine Activity and Rational Choice*, Vol. 5, pp. 259–294. New Brunswick: Transaction Publishers, 1993.

Cohen, L.E. and M. Felson, Social change and crime rate trends: A Routine Activity Approach. *American Sociological Review,* 44, pp. 588–608, 1979.

Cornish, D. and R. Clarke, *The Reasoning Criminal: Rational Choice Perspectives on Offending*. New York: Springer, 1986.

Craglia, M., R. Haining and P. Wiles, A comparative evaluation of approaches to urban crime pattern analysis. *Urban Studies*, 37(4), pp. 711–729, 2000.

Ekblom, P., Getting the best out of crime analysis. *Police Research Group: Crime Prevention Unit Series,* 10, pp. 1–42, 1988.

Fischer, M.M., H.J. Scholten and D. Unwin, Geographic information systems, spatial data analysis and spatial modelling: An introduction. In: M.M. Fischer, H.J. Scholten and D. Unwin (Eds), *Spatial Analytical Perspectives on GIS*, pp. 3–19. London: Taylor and Francis, 1996.

Flood, B., Strategic aspects of the UK National Intelligence Model. In: J.H. Ratcliffe (Ed.), *Strategic Thinking in Criminal Intelligence*, pp. 37–52. Sydney: Federation Press, 2004.

Fotheringham, A.S., C. Brunsdon and M. Charlton, *Geographically Weighted Regression*. Chichester: Wiley, 2002.

Gatrell, A.C. and C.E. Dunn, Geographical information systems and spatial epidemiology: Modelling the possible association between cancer of the larynx and incineration in North-East England. In: M.J.C. DeLepper, H.J. Scholten and R.M. Stern (Eds), *The Added Value of Geographical Information Systems in Public and Environmental Health*, pp. 215–235. London: Kluwer Academic Publishers, 1995.

Gill, P., *Rounding up theUusual Suspects? Developments in Contemporary Law Enforcement Intelligence*. Aldershot: Ashgate, 2000.

Goldstein, H., *Problem-Orientated Policing*. New York: McGraw-Hill, 1990.

Harries, K., *Mapping Crime: Principles and Practice*. Washington DC: US Department of Justice, 1999.

Hirschfield, A., P. Brown and P. Todd, GIS and the analysis of spatially-referenced crime data: Experiences in Merseyside, UK. *International Journal of Geographical Information Systems,* 9(2), pp. 191–210, 1995.

HMIC, *Northamptonshire Police: Intelligence Led Policing and Proactive Investigation of Crime*. London: Her Majesty's Inspectorate of Constabulary, 2001.

ICJIA, *STAC User Manual*. Chicago: Illinois Criminal Justice Information Authority, 1996.

Jeffery, C.R. and D.L. Zahm, Crime prevention through environmental design, opportunity theory, and rational choice models. In: R.V. Clarke and M. Felson (Eds), *Routine Activity and Rational Choice,* 323–350. New Brunswick: Transaction Publishers, 1993.

LaVigne, N.G. and E.R. Groff, The evolution of crime mapping in the United States. In: A. Hirschfield and K. Bowers (Eds), *Mapping and Analysing Crime Data*, pp. 203–221. London: Taylor and Francis, 2001.

Mayne, S.R., *Instructions and Orders*. London: Metropolitan Police, 1829.

McDowell, D., *Strategic Intelligence: A Handbook for Practitioners, Managers and Users*. Cooma: Istana Enterprises, 1998.

McGuire, P.G., The New York Police Department COMPSTAT Process. In: V. Goldsmith, P.G. McGuire, J.H. Mollenkopf and T.A. Ross (Eds), *Analyzing Crime Patterns: Frontiers of Practice,* pp. 11–22. Thousand Oaks: Sage, 2000.

McLafferty, S., D. Williamson, J.H. Mollenkopf and T.A. Ross, Identifying crime hot spots using kernel smoothing. In: V. Goldsmith, P.G. McGuire, J.H. Mollenkopf and T.A. Ross

(Eds), *Analyzing Crime Patterns: Frontiers of Practice*, pp. 77–85. Thousand Oaks: Sage, 2000.

NCIS, *The National Intelligence Model*. London: National Criminal Intelligence Service, 2000.

Nelson, A.L., R.D.F. Bromley and C.J. Thomas, Identifying micro-spatial and temporal patterns of violent crime and disorder in the British city centre. *Applied Geography*, 21(3), pp. 249–274, 2001.

Newman, G., Introduction: Towards a theory of situational crime prevention. In: G. Newman, R. Clarke and S.G. Shoham (Eds), *Rational Choice and Situational Crime Prevention: Theoretical Foundations*, pp. 1–23. Dartmouth: Ashgate, 1997.

NZP, *Briefing to the Incoming Minister*.Wellington: New Zealand Police 2002 (http://www.police.govt.nz/resources/2002/bim/bim.php).

Openshaw, S., GIS crime and GIS criminality. *Environment and Planning A*, 25(4), pp. 451–458, 1993.

Openshaw, S., A. Cross, M. Charlton and C. Brunsdon, *Lessons Learnt from a Post Mortem of a Failed GIS*. 2nd National Conference and Exhibition of the AGI, Brighton, October 1990.

Ratcliffe, J.H., On the accuracy of TIGER-type geocoded address data in relation to cadastral and census areal units. *International Journal of Geographical Information Science*, 15(5), pp. 473–485, 2001.

Ratcliffe, J.H., Aoristic signatures and the temporal analysis of high volume crime patterns. *Journal of Quantitative Criminology*, 18(1), pp. 23–43, 2002.

Ratcliffe, J.H., Intelligence-led policing. *Trends and Issues in Crime and Criminal Justice*, 248, Australian Institute of Criminology, 2003.

Ratcliffe, J.H., The Hotspot Matrix: A framework for the spatio-temporal targeting of crime reduction. *Police Practice and Research*, 5(1), pp. 7–25, 2004a.

Ratcliffe, J.H. (Ed.), *Strategic Thinking in Criminal Intelligence*. Sydney: Federation Press, 2004b.

Ratcliffe, J.H. and M.J. McCullagh, Hotbeds of crime and the search for spatial accuracy. *Geographical Systems*, 1(4), pp. 385–398, 1999.

Rengert, G.F., The journey to crime: Conceptual foundations and policy implications. In: D.J. Evans, N.R. Fyfe and D.T. Herbert (Eds), *Crime, Policing and Place: Essays in Environmental Criminology*, pp. 109–117. London: Routledge, 1992.

Rich, T.F., *The Use of Computerized Mapping in Crime Control and Prevention Programs*. Washington, DC: National Institute of Justice, 1995.

Robinson, M.B., Lifestyles, routine activities, and residential burglary victimization. *Journal of Crime and Justice*, 22(1), pp. 27–56, 1999.

Rossmo, D.K., Overview: Multivariate spatial profiles as a tool in crime investigation. In: C. Block, M. Daboub and S. Fregly (Eds), *Crime Analysis Through Computer Mapping*, pp. 65–97. Chicago: PERF, 1995a.

Rossmo, D.K., Place, space, and police investigations: Hunting serial violent criminals. In: D. Weisburd and J.E. Eck (Eds), *Crime and Place*, pp. 217–235. Monsey: Criminal Justice Press, 1995b.

Rossmo, D.K., Geographic profiling. In: J.L. Jackson and D.A. Bekerian (Eds), *Offender Profiling: Theory, Research and Practice*, pp. 159–175. New York: Wiley, 1997.

Rossmo, D.K., *Geographic Profiling*. Boca Raton: CRC Press, 2000.

Santtila, P., A. Zappalà, M. Laukkanenc and M. Picozzi, Testing the utility of a geographical profiling approach in three rape series of a single offender: A case study. *Forensic Science International*, 131(1), pp. 42–52, 2003.

Scott, M.S., *Problem-Oriented Policing: Reflections on the First 20 Years*.Washington, DC: COPS Office, 2000.

Sherman, L.W., D. Gottfredson, D. MacKenzie, J. Eck, P. Reuter and S. Bushway, *Preventing Crime: What Works, What Doesn't, What's Promising.* Washington, DC: National Institute of Justice, 1998.

Tilley, N., *Problem-Oriented Policing, Intelligence-Led Policing and the National Intelligence Model.* London: Jill Dando Institute of Crime Science, 2003.

Walsh,W.F., Compstat: An analysis of an emerging police managerial paradigm. *Policing: An International Journal of Police Strategies & Management,* 24(3), pp. 347–362, 2001.

Weisburd, D., *Translating Research Into Practice: Reflections on the Diffusion of Innovation in Crime Mapping.* Dallas: International Crime Mapping Research Conference, Texas, CMRC: NIJ, 2001.

Weisburd, D. and L. Green, Policing drug hot spots: The Jersey City drug market analysis experiment. *Justice Quarterly,* 12(4), pp. 711–735, 1995.

Weisburd, D., L. Maher, L. Sherman, M. Buerger, E. Cohn and A. Petrisino, Contrasting crime general and crime specific theory: The case of hot spots of crime. In: F. Alder and W.S. Laufer (Eds), *New Directions in Criminological Theory. Advances in Criminological Theory,* Vol. 4, pp. 45–70. London: Transaction Publishers, 1993.

Weisburd, D. and T. McEwen, Introduction: Crime mapping and crime prevention. In: D. Weisburd and T. McEwen (Eds), *Crime Mapping and Crime Prevention,* Vol. 8, pp. 1–23. New York: Criminal Justice Press, 1997.

Whyte, D., *Behind the Line of Truncheons': Crimes of the Powerful and the Policing of Valid Knowledge.* British Criminology Conference, Keele: The British Society of Criminology, 2003.

Wiles, P. and A. Costello, *The 'road to nowhere': The Evidence for Travelling Criminals.* London: Research, Development and Statistics Directorate (Home Office), 2000.

Yokota, K. and S.Watanabe, Computer-based retrieval of suspects using similarity of *modus operandi. International Journal of Police Science and Management,* 4(1), pp. 5–15, 2002.

CHAPTER 12

SOME REFLECTIONS ON DRUGS AND CRIME RESEARCH IN AN INTERNATIONAL CONTEXT

Sandeep Chawla[*]

INTRODUCTION

This paper[1] offers some reflections on how to develop more effective policies against crime[2], drawing on more than 10 years of research experience on the international drug problem. The paper consists of three parts. First, it tries to illustrate the so-called 'justice gap' in the world, and explain why an institution such as the United Nations has a comparative advantage in trying to close that gap. Secondly, it will detail four lessons that I have learnt from my own personal experience as head of research in the United Nations International Drug Control Programme, now called the United Nations Office on Drugs and Crime. Thirdly, it will try and show how these lessons can be applied in related areas and used as good practice in research on crime.

THE JUSTICE GAP

Figure 1 shows data on fraud from two sets of surveys, the United Nations (UN) Survey on Crime Trends and the Operations of Criminal Justice Systems (UNWCTS) and the International Crime Victim Survey (ICVS). The left scale is from the UNWCTS and the bars on the left scale show rates of fraud per 100,000 of the population.[3] The right

This chapter was previously published in *European Journal on Criminal Policy and Research* **10**: 85–98, 2004.

[*]   The views expressed in this paper are those of the author, and do not necessarily reflect those of the United Nations.

[1]   Based on a paper originally presented at the International Conference on Crime and Technology: New Frontiers for Legislation, Law Enforcement and Research, Courmayeur, Italy, 28–30 November 2003. Because it contains several personal reflections, a colloquial style has been maintained in some sections of the paper.

[2]   I am grateful to my colleague, Anna Alvazzi del Frate, for her advice on the sections of this paper dealing with crime issues.

[3]   The definition of fraud in the UNWCTS is 'Acquisition of another person's property by deception.'

Ernesto U. Savona (ed.), Crime and Technology: New Frontiers for Regulations, Law Enforcement and Research, 129–140.

FIGURE 1. Rates of fraud reported to the police and percentages of respondents who experienced consumer fraud, by world regions, 2000.

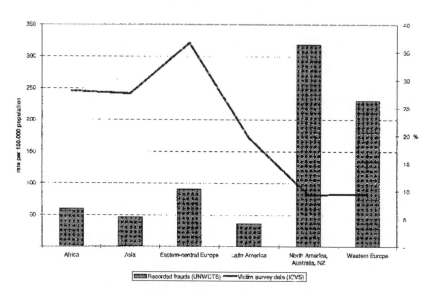

scale, which is the line on the graph, shows percentage of ICVS respondents who were victims of consumer fraud or cheating.[4] The reporting of fraud in North America, Australia, New Zealand and Western Europe is very high; however, the percentage of people who were victimized by consumer fraud is much lower. The left side of the graph shows quite clearly that the reporting of fraud is very low in Asia, Africa, Central and Eastern Europe and Latin America, but a lot more people in those regions were victims of fraud.

The figure is a good illustration of a justice gap. Despite so much discussion and rhetoric about the instruments of human rights and development, the realities are very far away. In many developing and transition countries, large numbers of people have no access to the instruments of justice and therefore no recourse if they are victimized. It is quite clear that the UN must address this justice gap. What the UN must do, if represented graphically in Figure 1, is simple: concentrate on the left side of the graph, lower the victimization line or increase the bars of recorded fraud. In other words, improve access to justice and get reporting systems working in the developing and transition countries, so that such large numbers of people do not feel victimized and have access to the instruments of justice. Now this is what the UN can do, ought to do, and is indeed obliged to do.

When one leaves the comfortable abstractions of the chart and enters the uncomfortable reality that the data is meant to represent, a serious problem becomes

---

4   The ICVS question is, 'Were you the victim of a consumer fraud? In other words, has someone when selling something to you or delivering a service cheated you in terms of quantity or quality of the goods/service?'.

apparent. Even if access to instruments of justice increased and the perception of victimization showed a commensurate decline, how would one measure these phenomena? One could use the same measures that are shown on the chart. Yet, more often than not, these numbers are hard to find, either because they are not counted, or because they are not reported and published. This leads to the first of the lessons which I have learnt from several years of leading research on drugs at the UN.

FOUR LESSONS

Measure, Count, and Keep Counting

When we speak of illegal drugs and the drug problem, we are really speaking of three phenomena: the production of the illicit drugs, their trafficking and their consumption. In other words, what drugs and how many of them are produced; how they are trafficked from the producer to the consumer; how many people consume them and how much they consume. Now, if we know what is produced and consumed, then trafficking is an automatically generated number, simply linking the production to the consumption. The problem, however, is that we do not know surely how much is produced. Even less certain is what is consumed. The oldest and most reliable data set in the drug field is on trafficking: seizures of illicit drugs by enforcement authorities. These numbers have been measured and reported since the international drug control system began early in the 20th century. Unfortunately, seizures are the most indirect of indicators to establish production or consumption. They only reveal a partial reality: how much of a particular drug was seized at a particular time. From the number of seizures, we have to extrapolate how much was produced and how much was consumed.

There is no rigorous scientific basis for that extrapolation. In the first half of the 20th century, law enforcement agencies used to have a golden rule. It was called 'the ten percent rule'. It was based on the assumption that 90% of total illicit drug production got through to consumers, and only 10% of it was seized – the interception rate (the proportion of total production that is seized). This is not valid any more. For the main drugs (heroin and cocaine) we have seen interception rates of 30% to 40% over the last 10 to 15 years. Unfortunately, this interception rate is frequently misunderstood. While over long periods of time, like a decade, the trend of seizures – whether they go up or down – does correlate positively with the trend of production and consumption, the interception rate, though often used as such, is not an indicator of law enforcement effectiveness. It is more likely to be an indicator of law enforcement priorities. For instance, in a number of Western Europe countries, seizure rates for cannabis have recently been going down. This does not mean that less cannabis is being trafficked or consumed. We know for a fact that more cannabis is being consumed. Yet if enforcement authorities put less priority on cannabis, they will seize less, and if they put more priority on cocaine and heroin, they will seize more. Now, the fact that this priority changes tells us something about drug policy, but it tells us nothing about the size of total production and consumption, which still have to be extrapolated, or established by other methods.

We do, indeed, measure production and consumption by other means, but the results are not very robust. The production of the main plant-based drugs, cocaine and heroin, can be estimated by measuring the extent of coca bush and opium poppy cultivation. This is done by standard agricultural survey methods, combining land surveys with satellite monitoring. Once the area of cultivation has been measured, it can be multiplied by a yield factor to give an estimate of the total amount of the drug produced. The term 'estimate' is used because there are many uncertainties in the process. First, the activity is generally illegal, so peasants or farmers will not divulge the information willingly. Secondly, once the area has been estimated, the yield must be established. How much opium, for instance, can be harvested from x number of hectares of opium poppy cultivation? These yields vary from 10 to 50 kg of opium per hectare. They are lower when the poppy is grown on rain-fed land, such as in Myanmar, and higher when it is grown on irrigated land, such as in Afghanistan. Thirdly, a conversion factor has to be established to estimate how much heroin can be derived from a unit of opium. This is generally assumed to be 1:10, i.e. 1 kg of heroin from 10 kg of opium, but it also varies and depends upon where the opium poppy is being cultivated. Similar uncertainties exist when trying to estimate the total amount of cocaine that can be produced from coca bush cultivation. For cannabis, we are even further away because we do not even have global estimates of how much of it grows wild, or how much is cultivated. Measurement is also difficult for synthetic drugs. Most of them do not have an easily identifiable botanical starting material. They are made from chemicals, called 'precursors' in the trade, which often have a wide range of industrial and medical uses. Quite apart from the regulatory problem of establishing effective controls over the illicit use of substances with so many legitimate uses, there is also a considerable measurement problem. It is hard to establish how much of a particular chemical is diverted for the manufacture of an illicit drug, particularly when the total production volume of the chemical is so large, and the amount diverted so small. Even if we know the amount of precursors seized, or prevented from diversion into illicit channels, we still have the extrapolation problem noted above for the plant-based drugs.

Having established the seizure and production totals, one enters the most difficult terrain: estimating the number of users. Enter the epidemiologist and the survey researcher, whose work is used more and more to try and estimate the numbers of people who use drugs, the incidence and the prevalence of drug abuse. This is harder than it sounds for the obvious reason that since the activity is generally illegal, it is in the interests of the user to conceal rather than reveal it. Complex methods of measurement, ranging from surveys of invisible populations to cross-checking registry data from hospitals, treatment centres, police stations and courts of law, have consequently been developed. The measures are all imperfect, and most suffer from the problem of comparability, because the phenomena (an arrest, a hospital emergency room episode) are so different. After much methodological juggling, however, it is possible to arrive at an estimate of the number of drug users. Then it becomes a matter of triangulating the three numbers: the estimates of production, trafficking and consumption. This is a nightmare, because they do not always tally. It is at this point that science needs to be supplemented by art, and tempered by policy relevance. The former means using the intuitions and hunches of experts who have a 'feel' for the data. The latter means accepting the necessity of producing a number, or estimate, which is derived as rigorously and transparently as possible, because that is always better than the 'back-of-the-envelope' estimate delivered off-the-cuff.[5] This, then, is the first lesson: *measure the central phenomena, count them where you can, keep counting them and make quality improvements gradually and incrementally over time.*

Publish or Perish, Either in Inter-Governmental Default, or in Public Hysteria

With both drugs and crime, there is a well-known dilemma of trying to control global problems with systems of control that are territorially bound. This is a frequently discussed issue; drug and crime problems are not territorially bound, but the control systems are. Even though we have international instruments to prevent and control them, the jurisdictions of control tend to be territorial and national. The result is that problems like this are perpetually spinning out of the national arena onto new areas and spaces where international controls are simply not quick enough or deep enough to control them. To adapt Max Weber's celebrated typology, the regulator is condemned to be perpetually behind the entrepreneur. Now, nearly a century after Weber developed the concept,[6] it is still valid, but more complicated. Globalization makes it difficult to distinguish the legal from the illegal, particularly when a certain activity may be illegal in a national context, but legal, or at any rate unclearly defined, in an international context.

Some examples from international drug debates, articulated hypothetically to maintain political correctness, can illustrate this. Country A has a large problem with the consumption of a particular drug – cocaine or heroin. Country B produces a lot of that cocaine or heroin. Country A says to Country B, 'Stop your production and supply, because my poor people are getting addicted and dying.' Country B says to Country A, 'Stop your consumption, because your demand is pulling and sustaining my supply.' The result is often a deadlock, because it is not easy to establish the extent to which a market is supply or demand-driven. This is further complicated by the fact that the trafficker who links the supply and demand may not be from Country A or B, and may be from Country C, or may use the territory of Country C to move the drugs from producer to consumer. In such a case, both Country A and Country B may turn to Country C and say, 'You are the cause of the problem; if only you could stop your traffickers, or trafficking, we would solve the problem.' The deadlock only worsens, fingers are pointed, acrimonious debates multiply,

---

5   This is not to demean the importance of qualitative research on the long-term or unintended effects of particular policies; it is only to assert that this kind of research is better done in academic institutions where the demand for quantitative estimates is less pressing than it is in public organizations, national or international.

6   See Rheinstein (1968), and Gerth and Wright Mills (1958).

solving the problem recedes further and further into the background and the whole situation begins to resemble a theatre of the absurd. This is what was characterized above as *inter-governmental default*.

Drugs and crime are issues that *ipso facto* generate considerable amounts of public anxiety and moral panic. What happens, then, in a world in which there is more and more information overload and less and less reliance on knowledge? Information is instant; knowledge comes more slowly, growing out of the painstaking process of assimilating and analysing a great deal of information. It is obviously easier to get instant information than to build knowledge. It is easier, and quicker, in contemporary parlance, to 'see the film' rather than 'read the book'. It is easier to get the gist of an issue from the little sound-bytes of information than turn up as newspapers headlines, rather than go deeply into the issue in all its complexity. If hundreds of such sound-bytes are competing for the short attention span of a passive audience, then it is obvious that the most entertaining or sensational bits will win the battle for attention. There is thus ever more sensational reportage of drugs and crime issues. This exacerbates public anxiety, creates moral panic and makes public debate increasingly unhelpful in terms of finding real solutions. Here are the conditions for what was characterized above as *public hysteria*.

One practical way out of these two problems of inter-governmental default and public hysteria is to try and change the terms of the discourse – to actually go out and publish systematically the numbers that come from the counting described in the first lesson above. The numbers and estimates should be published and put before public scrutiny. This would leave people to draw their own conclusions, as well as create a publicly accessible evidence-base to inform both discourse and policy. Quantitative estimates of the size of the drug problem, when published and put before public scrutiny, will balance the limitations of decisions being based exclusively on inter-governmental debate, or on short-term political responses to public anxiety. One example should suffice. For more than thirty years, the United Nations Commission on Narcotic Drugs, the inter-governmental body responsible for drug control, reviewed annual reports on illicit drug trafficking and abuse. These reports contained very valuable data on different dimensions of the drug problem provided to the United Nations by its states members. Yet there was no global aggregation of this data. Though reports to inter-governmental bodies of the United Nations are publicly accessible, the UN did not *publish* periodic overviews of the world drug problem. There was thus no objective, internationally balanced source of information: some governments produced national assessments of the drug problem as they perceived it, and a lot of journalists produced a lot of news stories that usually reflected only a partial reality. In 1997, the UN International Drug Control Programme, now called the UN Office on Drugs and Crime, published a *World Drug Report* (UNDCP 1997). It contained the first global estimates of illicit drug production, trafficking and consumption. Though some of the numbers were contested – what first estimate, particularly of an illegal activity, is not? – the Report was popular, well reviewed, and seemed to fulfil a public need for balanced information in several parts of the world. Building upon this, and a special session of the UN General Assembly that called for reliable information on the world drug problem, the UN produced a statistical analysis in a publication called

Global Illicit Drug Trends in 1999 (for the latest in this series, see UNODC 2003a). This has become an annual publication, been produced every year since 1999, and is now widely regarded as the standard source of statistical reference on the drug problem. This is a result of counting and of publishing the counts. The second lesson, therefore, is to *publish or perish, either in inter-governmental default, or in public hysteria.*

Limit the Dangers of Committing the 'Euphemistic Fallacy'

The third lesson is to limit the dangers of committing what one might call the 'euphemistic fallacy'. The phrase is adapted from an old debate in moral philosophy about the so-called 'naturalistic fallacy'.[7] A euphemism is a polite way of expressing a hard reality, a mild expression that is less harsh, but also less precise, than the one it replaces. Thus, rather than saying that so and so 'died', the euphemism is that so and so 'passed away'. We live in an age of euphemism. It is all pervasive. For example, we would not, in politically correct discourse, speak of a 'poor country'. The euphemism, earlier, was to call it an 'under-developed country'. Even that was too blunt, so we got another, even less accurate euphemism: a 'developing country'. So, poor country, under-developed country, developing country, are all supposed to mean the same thing, but we get progressively less accurate as we move along the path of euphemism.

One particularly difficult euphemism of our time is the term 'terrorism'. It is, in a certain sense, an extreme euphemism, because terrorism is not an objectively verifiable phenomenon. What is objectively verifiable about the thing that is called terrorism is that it claims civilian or non-combatant lives, which can be counted and measured. Most of the other things that are commonly called terrorism are hard to count and measure. There is a well-known and much quoted genre of examples: today's respectable national leader could well have been yesterday's terrorist. There are several countries in the world whose legitimate leaders were earlier called 'terrorists'.

To offer a more concrete, and personal, example: when I began to do research for my PhD on British imperial history, one of the things I was looking at was imperial responses to Indian nationalism. I went to archives and public records in New Delhi and London. When I looked up the subject indexes of government files and records, I was horrified that I could find virtually nothing under the category of 'nationalism'. One does not have to be a historian to know that the Indian national movement was a defining theme of imperial de-colonisation in the first half of the 20th century. Yet Indian nationalism did not appear in the indexes of government archives. Eventually, like many other researchers, I did find the voluminous documentation on Indian nationalism, but it was all neatly assembled under categories such as 'sedition', 'terrorism', 'agitation' or simply 'public nuisance'. These were the terms in which British colonial administrators saw the Indian movement to end British imperial rule in India.

---

7   First suggested by the British philosopher, G.E. Moore in *Principia Ethica* in 1903. The only way to recognize moral 'goodness' was by intuition; if one attempted to identify it with a certain natural property, such as pleasure, then one was committing the 'naturalistic fallacy'.

For the imperial administrator to call that movement 'nationalism' would have been an extreme euphemism. Such are the problems of time-bound terminologies and terms like 'terrorism' do not mean much until we can contextualise them. Unless we contextualise, therefore, we commit the 'euphemistic fallacy'. If we do, we limit the utility of our research, because flawed questions will only give flawed answers.

In one of the presentations to the conference for which the present paper was originally prepared, the following statement was made: 'The international community needs to criminalise computer related abuse'. When confronted with a prescriptive statement of this nature, one cannot help but draw a parallel with the drug problem. If one replaced the phrase 'computer related abuse' with the phrase 'drug abuse', the statement would be 'The international community needs to criminalise drug abuse'. This has doubtlessly been asserted many times. Yet some of the most difficult and vexatious debates in drug policy today are over precisely this question of the international community criminalizing or de-criminalizing drug abuse. The debates are rendered more difficult by the fact that the *use* of an illicit drug is seldom a criminal offense, but the *possession* of an illicit drug is a criminal offense. To distinguish between users and dealers/traffickers, some countries establish a threshold quantity; a person will only be prosecuted for possession if found with a quantity that exceeds the threshold. Drug abuse is measurable at least to the extent that illicit drugs have a definite pharmacological effect. Even if it were definable, 'computer-related abuse' is certainly not measurable. If 'computer-related abuse' were to become a criminal offense in a law against cyber-crime, how would we prosecute it when we have no means of measuring it? This is what happens when the frontiers between advocacy (which is necessary to get new, previously unconsidered issues on to a policy agenda) and policy are not clearly defined. The confusion is perpetuated when there is a requirement to make 'evidence-based' policy, and to use evidence to assess policy. The only way out is to try and avoid the euphemistic fallacy. Our institutions and policies may require us to use euphemisms, but that is no reason for our research questions to be euphemistic and therefore difficult to answer.

There is another debate in drug policy, which offers an illustration – 'harm reduction'. The term, in itself, is innocuous. In the context of drug policy, however, it becomes loaded (UNDCP 1997: 188). This is because some countries avow it and others abjure it. The divergence, however, is not about actual drug control measures, but more about the ultimate purpose of drug policy. The countries which avow harm-reduction argue that some people in society will always use drugs, and policy should concentrate on containing the negative consequences (crime, HIV/AIDS) of that drug use. The countries which abjure harm reduction argue that society should not tolerate any drug use at all, and government endorsement of policies to contain the negative consequences of drug use (like distributing clean needles) would mean implicit tolerance of that drug use. Resolving a debate that involves such different philosophical positions may not be easy and the result is often inter-governmental deadlock. Such an impasse need not deter the researcher who, by avoiding the euphemistic fallacy, would ignore the term 'harm reduction', and concentrate on drug-related mortality and morbidity, and the relationship between injecting drug use and blood borne diseases. These are consequences of drug use. They can be counted and measured. The numbers can be reported and published without any reference to harm reduction. Avoiding the euphemistic fallacy thus enables the defusing and demystifying of a vexatious debate.

Returning to a problem that was identified earlier, one frequently asked question today is whether there is documentary evidence of the links between drug trafficking and terrorism, to show how trafficking finances terrorism. Everybody knows that there is a connection, it is common sense, and there is a lot of anecdotal, and even some historical, information on it. Unfortunately there is no contemporary documentary evidence, at least not of the kind that would satisfy the most basic of scientific standards. The third lesson, *limiting the dangers of committing the 'euphemistic fallacy'*. therefore means, in this context, to de-construct the concepts of terrorism and drug trafficking into definable phenomena which we can count (such as the number of civilian casualties, production volumes of drugs and their wholesale and retail prices); and then use the resulting estimates to build an evidence-base for policy.

Divorce Research and Policy, Because Research Is Policy-Dependent; Make Research Policy-Relevant, and Re-marry It to Policy

Finally, the fourth lesson is to institute a divorce between research and policy and to re-marry them under different conditions. The divorce is needed because at the moment research is too policy-*dependent*. It needs to become policy-*relevant*. This distinction is not as obscure as it may *prima facie* appear to be. In the context of inter-national organizations working within the frameworks of multilateral control systems such as drug control, there are certain special conditions. They are best illustrated by two assertions – some might call them platitudes – often made about the UN. The first one is, 'The UN is nothing more than a mirror of its states members.' The second one is: 'A chain is no stronger than its weakest link.' Both statements reflect a unique reality of the UN in our contemporary world. The UN can seldom act independent of its states members and is often hamstrung when there are fundamental disagreements between them. Since states collectively form the chain of any multilateral system such as the UN, any one state deviating from the norm, or defying it, will compromise the whole system. I have written a detailed account elsewhere about what this means for drug control (Chawla 2004). For the purposes of this paper, it is sufficient to argue that the *political* process of dealing with a state that deviates from the multilateral norm has to be separated from the *knowledge-building* process that would enable one to understand the roots of the deviation. The latter process is what I would charac-terize as policy-*relevant* research.

A few examples would illustrate. Until very recently, Afghanistan has been a weak link in the multilateral chain. More than three decades of endemic conflict, ranging from foreign occupation to civil war, made it into a haven for anything illegal and beyond the rule of law such as drug production, trafficking and the arms trade. The Afghan state has been variously described as 'weak', 'compromised', or 'failed'. Whatever the description, and this issue is not without controversy, what is clear is that Afghanistan became a space which was hospitable to anything that could not thrive where there was a rule of law. Such spaces exist within several countries of the world, particularly in situations of civil war, but it is not often that a whole country gets into such a situation and remains in it for so long. It is no wonder, then, that Afghanistan became the source of three-quarters of the heroin produced in the world. This production had to be measured and tracked in order to give the international (i.e. multilateral) community some idea about the supply of the world's most dangerous illicit drug. Thus, every year since 1994, the UN has done an annual survey of opium cultivation in Afghanistan and published the results (for the latest one, see UNODC 2003b). The UN has also published an extensive study on the origins, dimensions and consequences of the opium economy in Afghanistan (UNODC 2003c). Work of this kind is policy-*relevant*, because it provides an evidence-base on which policy can be made or assessed.

Investigating the origins of a particular problem, particularly when it is a social problem like drugs or crime, usually involves historical investigation. The writing of history can become very policy-*dependent*, because even though it is about the past, history serves the needs of the present. 'All history', goes a celebrated dictum attributed to the Italian philosopher, Benedetto Croce (1886–1952), 'is contemporary history'. Because drugs are such an emotive issue in our contemporary world, the historiography of drug policy is very sparse, full of gaps and badly in need of development (Berridge 1996; Chawla 2004: 236–238). The result is that so much of today's discourse on drugs appears to proceed in blithe ignorance of even the most elementary historical understanding. Several critiques of international drug policy thus record, somewhat triumphantly, the discovery that the United States of America is the champion of what is called the 'global prohibition regime' (Nadelmann 1990). Quite apart from the misrepresentation of a regulatory regime as a prohibitionist one (Chawla 2004: 242–243), it is almost a truism to state that the major power of a particular age is the champion of the international *status quo* at that time. Taking another example, a lack of historical knowledge could well lead to an assertion that the British Empire was the first cartel for both drug and human trafficking. Of course it was not. When British ships carried slaves across the Atlantic in the 17th century, it was not called 'human trafficking'; it was called 'slavery' and it was not illegal. It was also that same British Empire which later abolished slavery and then did so much to stop it in the world. When opium was transported to China, the British, and indeed the international system of the 19th century which they dominated, called it 'free trade'. Besides that, opium was not illegal at that time. China tried to make it so, but China was put under the duress of the major powers of the time to accept 'free trade' in opium. It was only in the early 20th century that what the Chinese had been arguing for over a hundred years was accepted and the opium trade was made illegal. Therefore, if the history of drug problems is written from the point of view of legitimating or justifying particular policies, we might call it policy-*dependent*. If, however, it were written from the point of view of building a knowledge base to understand a contemporary situation, we might call it policy-*relevant* (cf. UNODC 2003c: 81–95). The fourth lesson, in summary, is *to divorce research and policy (because much research is policy-dependent); to make research policy-relevant; and then re-marry it to policy.*

GOOD PRACTICE IN RESEARCH ON CRIME

How can research contribute to more effective policies against crime? I ask the indulgence of experts for my temerity in addressing this issue. I am not a criminologist, but, to take an analogy from Ronald Clarke, I do know a bit more about 'crime science' than 'criminology'.[8] That, coupled with what I have recounted above about my experience with the drug issue, would appear to indicate three kinds of good practice in the future. The first concerns the crime data that the UN gathers from the two surveys on Crime Trends and Criminal Justice systems, and on Victims of Crime. Each of the four lessons described above can be applied to these data-sets: count, publish the results, avoid the euphemistic fallacy, and make the research policy-relevant. This is not to say that these things are not being done already; it is to assert, rather, that they can be done more carefully and systematically. An articulated plan is always better than an implicit one. We should continue the incremental process of improving the quality of the survey instruments, increase the frequency of the surveys, and speed up the turn-around time for analysing them and publishing their results. Though it may take some time and resources to accomplish, we ought to aim to do each of these surveys annually.

Secondly, we can enrich research and the evidence-base for crime prevention and criminal justice by better working relationships between the UN and the international network of criminal justice research institutes. Such relationships could be defined by a research agenda, with each party doing what it has comparative advantage to do, replacing policy-dependent research and technical assistance projects with policy-relevant ones, and sharing the responsibility – perhaps on a regional basis – of publishing research findings. The quinquennial crime congresses could then become occasions for policy development based upon analysis of longer-term trends.

Thirdly, we will need a lot of hard work to build data-sets and statistics on all of the new areas where international legislation is being, or has only recently been developed: the new UN Conventions on Corruption and on Transnational Organised Crime. We cannot even estimate the real size and extent of these problems because there is such a lack of hard numbers and quantitative data to so. To get the data, we ought to try and adapt the two existing surveys rather than add to the widely acknowledged problem of proliferating survey instruments. As we develop these data-sets, we will have to watch for the many pitfalls, the most dangerous of which is the euphemistic fallacy. It is only by means such as these that we can highlight and eventually close the justice gap described at the beginning of this paper, both in terms of balancing perception data with official records, as well as securing wider access, for the many that lack it, to the instruments of justice.

---

8   Ronald V. Clarke in Introduction to Session IV (New Challenges for Research), at the International Conference on Crime and Technology: New Frontiers for Legislation, Law Enforcement and Research, Courmayeur, Italy, 28–30 November 2003.

REFERENCES

Berridge, V., European drug policy: The need for historical perspectives. *European Addiction Research*, 3(2), pp. 219–225, 1996.

Chawla, S., Multilateral drug control. In: M. Vellinga (Ed.), *The Political Economy of the Drug Industry*, pp. 224–244. Gainesville: University Press of Florida, 2004.

Gerth, H.H. and C. Wright Mills (Trans. and Eds), *From Max Weber*. New York: Galaxy, 1958.

Nadelmann, E., Global prohibition regimes: The evolution of norms in international society. *International Organization*, 44(4), pp. 480–526, 1990.

Rheinstein, M. (Ed.), *Max Weber on Law in Economy and Society*. New York: Simon and Schuster, 1968.

United Nations International Drug Control Programme, UNDCP, *World Drug Report*. Oxford: Oxford University Press, 1997.

United Nations Office on Drugs and Crime (UNODC), *Global Illicit Drug Trends, 2003*. Vienna: United Nations, 2003a.

United Nations Office on Drugs and Crime (UNODC), *Afghanistan Opium Survey, October 2003*. Vienna: United Nations, 2003b.

United Nations Office on Drugs and Crime (UNODC), *The Opium Economy in Afghanistan*. Vienna: United Nations, 2003c.

THE AUTHORS

Lucie Angers is Senior Counsel of the Criminal Law Policy Section of Justice (Canada).

Neil Bailey is Director of Intelligence Services at the National Criminal Intelligence Service (NCIS) (United Kingdom).

Giuseppe Busia is Director of the Studies and Documentation Service of the Authority for the Protection of Personal Data (Italy).

Sandeep Chawla is Chief of the Policy Analysis and Research Branch of the United Nations Office on Drugs and Crime (UNODC) of Vienna (Austria).

Ronald V. Clarke is Professor of Criminology at the School of Criminal Justice of Rutgers University (USA).

Antonio M. Costa is Under-Secretary-General of the United Nations and Executive Director of United Nations Office on Drugs and Crime (UNODC) of Vienna (Austria).

Gloria Laycock is Professor of Crime Science at University College London and Director of the Jill Dando Institute of Crime Science of University College London (United Kingdom).

Mara Mignone was Researcher at TRANSCRIME, Joint Research Centre on Transnational Crime, Università di Trento – Università Cattolica di Milano (Italy), up to June 2004.

Christopher Painter is Deputy Chief of the Computer Crime and Intellectual Property Section (CCIPS) at the United States Department of Justice (USA) and Chair of the G8 High Tech Crime Sub Group of the Lyon Group.

Fausto Pocar is Professor of International Law at Milan University (Italy) and Vice President of the International Criminal Tribunal for the Former Yugoslavia (Netherlands).

Jerry H. Ratcliffe is Professor of Criminal Justice at Temple University (USA).

Guido Rossi is Chairman of ISPAC/Centro nazionale di prevenzione e difesa sociale (CNPDS) and Professor of Commercial Law at the Bocconi University of Milan (Italy).

Ernesto U. Savona is Professor of Criminology at the Università Cattolica di Milano and Director of TRANSCRIME, Joint Research Centre on Transnational Crime, Università di Trento – Università Cattolica di Milano (Italy).

Cindy J. Smith is Director of the Criminal Justice Graduate Programme, Division of Criminology, Criminal Justice and Social Policy at the University of Baltimore (USA).